UNNATURAL
HABITAT

UNNATURAL HABITAT

THE NATIVE
AND EXOTIC WILDLIFE
OF LOS ANGELES

CRAIG STANFORD

ILLUSTRATIONS BY
MADDALENA BEARZI

HEYDAY
50
Berkeley, California

Library of Congress Cataloging-in-Publication Data

Names: Stanford, Craig B. (Craig Britton), 1956- author. | Bearzi,
   Maddalena, illustrator.
Title: Unnatural habitat : the native and exotic wildlife of Los Angeles /
   Craig Stanford ; illustrations by Maddalena Bearzi.
Description: Berkeley, California : Heyday, [2024] | Includes
   bibliographical references.
Identifiers: LCCN 2023048844 (print) | LCCN 2023048845 (ebook) | ISBN
   9781597146395 (paperback) | ISBN 9781597146418 (epub)
Subjects: LCSH: Natural history--California--Los Angeles. | Biotic
   communities--California--Los Angeles. | Animals--California--Los
   Angeles. | Plants--California--Los Angeles. | Nature
   observation--California--Los Angeles. | Urban ecology
   (Biology)--California--Los Angeles.
Classification: LCC QH105.C2 S73 2024 (print) | LCC QH105.C2 (ebook) |
   DDC 578.09794/94--dc23/eng/20231213
LC record available at https://lccn.loc.gov/2023048844
LC ebook record available at https://lccn.loc.gov/2023048845

Cover Art: Adobe Stock/marchello74
Cover Design: Archie Ferguson
Interior Design/Typesetting: Faceout Studio, Paul Nielsen

Published by Heyday
P.O. Box 9145, Berkeley, California 94709
(510) 549-3564
heydaybooks.com

Printed in East Peoria, Illinois, by Versa Press, Inc.

10 9 8 7 6 5 4 3 2 1

For all those
devoted to preserving
wildness in our
Los Angeles area

CONTENTS

IV. BACKYARD VISITORS

V. REMARKABLE NEIGHBORS

The Hollow Ecosystem

I'm a biologist, and for thirty years I have lived in small suburban towns of the San Gabriel Valley, wedged against the mountains just north of Los Angeles. I was raised in a very different sort of American suburb: a little town in New Jersey just outside New York City. I grew up as a backyard naturalist keeping checklists of birds and salamanders, later expanding my horizons to local forests, ponds, and swamps. These adventures eventually led me to far-flung corners of the world, where I began a career studying the private lives of little-known animals in the tropics. When I moved to the Los Angeles basin, I discovered an ecosystem so bizarre, with its unique mosaic of native, nonnative, and invasive plants and animals, that many years later I'm still trying to understand it. This book is intended to help you understand it too.

This morning, as I walked out my front door, a flock of big, bright-green parrots swooped into my yard, squawking raucously: red-headed Amazons wheeling against the backdrop of the San Gabriel Mountains. I admired them for a minute, soaking in the bright Southern California sunshine. The air was then further split by a piercing mournful cry. A peacock was sitting calmly on a roof across the street. His flock was scattered across a couple of green lawns, peahens and their chicks scratching and pecking in the dirt and casually strolling between parked cars and palm trees. So far, a typical morning. I headed out for a walk toward the canyon entrance just up the street. As I reached it, I noticed a pack of four coyotes trotting casually down the street toward me. They were gorgeous, russet and gray, well fed and in peak condition. Seeing me, two peeled off while the others continued on, passing me casually no more than twenty feet away. I turned and noticed a lady walking two small dogs and called out to her that the coyotes were coming her way. She scrambled to pick up both dogs and moved to the far sidewalk, only to have the coyotes pass by her and her dogs, each group eyeing the other warily. It could have been much worse; coyotes have attacked and killed dogs in this scenario, even when their owners stood their ground to protect them.

This vignette of life in suburban Los Angeles unfolded in less than fifteen minutes. It's a beautiful, Edenic landscape by most standards, even in modest neighborhoods: full of green grass, brightly colored flowers, and towering shade trees. It also maintains a modicum of wildness. Last year a bobcat entered my neighbor's yard, killed a squirrel, climbed a backyard oak, and tore apart its breakfast while the family looked on. Bears leave the canyon and wander through our neighborhood, napping in backyards and dipping into swimming pools. Mountain lions occasionally stroll the streets backing up to the San Gabriels. And for every sighting of a native wild cat, canine, or hawk, there's another of an exotic animal that hails from the other side of the world but calls our neighborhood home.

Underlying the verdant suburban settings, environmental troubles abound. The exotic flowers and trees are like living mannequins. They're pretty, but they contribute little to the landscape as components of a healthy ecosystem. Some produce fruits or flowers that are used by hummingbirds, butterflies, and honeybees; most do not. Even those whose flowers feed our wildlife fail to feed the millions of insects that are dependent on particular native plants to complete their life cycles. Caterpillars usually specialize on certain plants. If we take those plants out of the ecosystem, the caterpillars that depend on them will disappear, and along with them the birds and other animals that depend on them for food. Our suburban ecosystem has, in a sense, collapsed, leaving only an outward appearance of Nature—and only as long as huge quantities of water are dumped on it regularly. It is hollow. The natural interactions among plants and animals that compose a healthy ecosystem are largely gone.

Southern California is not a landscape well suited to dense, sedentary human habitation. It's seasonally arid, and except for a few months of winter rain—which sometimes fail to arrive—water is at a premium. In 2021, the flames of more than eight thousand fires stretched their tentacles into more than four million acres of California forest and chapparal. That was nearly 4 percent of the land mass of the state. The fires were mostly sparked by lightning, fed by undergrowth that had not burned in many years, and fanned to explosive force by Santa Ana winds. The fires were ultimately fed by climate change, creating hotter tinderbox summers in this Mediterranean landscape.

The natural Southern California landscape is not the one in which most suburban Angelenos live. Most of us inhabit a verdant but ecologically hollow subtropical ecosystem, full of palms and exotic flowering plants from all over the world. Only the soil, the rocks, and the scattered majestic oak trees are natives, and the oaks are disappearing at a tragic rate. Suburbanites have replicated the green, grassy lawns and temperate-zone trees that they either grew up with or learned to value as the children or grandchildren of easterners. This lush green world can only be maintained with lots and lots of water, which must be poured onto a landscape that wants desperately to return to its natural semi-aridity. It has often been stated that Southern California lacks nearly everything people need; water, energy, and even soil are imported in large quantities. The early developers knew that to attract customers to build or buy homes, they had to change that perception and create the false appearance of lush landscape.

The collapsed nature of our hollowed-out ecosystem isn't easily visible. Block after block of well-planted gardens and shade trees create a facsimile of a vibrant, natural landscape. Underneath, there is a great emptiness. Unlike native plants that are adapted to seasonal drought and feed a rich community of insects—which in turn feed native birds and other animals—exotic plants don't feed many native insects, causing some to disappear. In their place, we have introduced creatures from all over the world: our honeybees, earthworms, and even many of our spiders are native to other continents. In the absence of the foods they need, native birds can't feed their young, and so their populations decline.

A few native species that adapt well to Los Angeles suburbia—coyotes, house finches, mockingbirds, to name a few—are more abundant than they'd be in Southern California's natural arid scrub environment. Other common species, like opossums and fox squirrels, don't belong in California; they were either brought here by well-intended people or arrived here on their own. The abundance of these few common species gives the misleading impression that animal and plant biodiversity in suburbia are thriving. Most native species with a narrower range of habitat needs have disappeared or cling to a precarious existence.

Natural ecosystems are extraordinarily complex. It takes decades to even begin to understand the pattern of nutrients and energy cycling through a community of plants and animals. Tropical rainforests are among the most intricate and complicated systems, natural or human-made, on the planet. The Los Angeles basin is an ecosystem too, a natural one overlaid by a profoundly unnatural one. But it's nevertheless an ecosystem. Like all habitats, it has many functioning parts, and an ecologist wants to understand how those parts fit together.

First is the environmental context: climate and topography. Southern California is often described as having a Mediterranean climate, with long, dry, hot summers followed by cool, rainy winters. We are subject to drought and fire, and our native plants have evolved to thrive under those conditions. The topography is characterized by rugged canyons and peaks, among which too many homeowners have built their abodes despite the eternal risk of fire, flood, and landslides. But it's the living world—the biosphere—of Los Angeles that makes it the place we all know.

Seasons in Southern California work differently than in many other parts of the world. The onset of our growing season is the start of the annual rains in late autumn. After a mild spring, the hot, dry months of July to October hit, and plant life just hangs on, waiting for life-giving rain to return. These summer months are to Southern California what winter months are to more northern climes. In the North, hostile temperatures and lack of water—other than ice and snow that last for months—have produced communities of plants and animals adapted to shut down their systems to survive the lean months. To a plant, a snowy winter is a drought, at least until the spring thaw arrives. A coniferous tree's needles are just leaves highly adapted to minimize water loss during a frozen winter. In the North, mammals go dormant, slowing their breathing and heart rate to survive a season when food is hard to find. Here in Southern California, animals do their best to avoid the intense heat by staying underground or foraging only at dawn and dusk, while trying to cope with the dearth of good food. Some reptiles estivate, shutting down their systems in much the way that mammals do while hibernating. When the autumn rains come, many animals magically appear to resume their active lives.

It takes some perspective-adjusting to appreciate our local environment. When family and friends visit from the East Coast in summer, they're disappointed by the barren brown hills. We experience what southwesterners euphemistically call a "dry heat." Autumn is also a dry and warm season. During my early years in California, I eagerly anticipated September as the harbinger of cooler weather that would usher in a crisp October. How wrong I was. September is one of the hottest months on the Southern California calendar, and early October is prone to furnace heat too. Californians know this is the fire season, when high temperatures combined with months without rain and Santa Ana winds create a tinderbox that can be lethal. Only later in October do daytime temperatures moderate and allow plants and animals to renew their seasonal lives.

The cool, wet winter months are a time when most outdoorsy Southern Californians feel renewed too. Gardens spring to life, the hills abruptly turn emerald green, and the air is fresh, the rain having pulled the summertime dust from it. Unless you're stuck on a flooded Los Angeles freeway, it's a wonderful time to live in Southern

California. The flowery color palette of suburban communities stands against a backdrop of snow-topped mountains. The ski slopes are an hour away, the desert is an hour and a half distant, and your background is fragrant with flowers as vivid as those of Monet's Giverny.

Though the overall climate of Southern California is considered Mediterranean, there are so many local variations that generalizations fail to capture the reality of living here. From my home in the San Gabriel Valley some forty kilometers from the coast, it's a forty-minute drive to the beach. On a hot August day when the sidewalks are sizzling and the air is over a hundred degrees Fahrenheit in Pasadena, the thermometer plummets to an equable seventy-two as the coast approaches. While the inland canyons are baking, the coastline is cloaked in a marine layer of clouds and mist that can be sweater weather. Giving gardening advice here means asking precisely where one lives, because microclimates vary so widely even from one town to the next.

In addition to the coast versus inland canyon differences, there are the mountains. From the Pacific coast eastward, the Santa Monica, San Gabriel, and San Bernadino Mountains loom over and around the Los Angeles basin. They provide the basin with its breathtaking backdrop on winter days, when the latter two ranges may be topped with snow. They also trap the emissions of millions of cars and trucks, creating a layer of smog pushed against their slopes by the oceans' onshore breezes.

My home is at the base of the San Gabriels—the foothills rise a few hundred meters from my front door. The San Gabriels are among the fastest-growing mountains on Earth, with peaks of 3,000 meters. The rugged San Bernadinos reach more than 3,500 meters, and one of its peaks, Mount San Gorgonio, is the highest point in Southern California, high enough to host popular ski resorts in winter.

The steep San Bernardino canyons were among the last places in Southern California where grizzly bears could be still found in the nineteenth century, and today they remain enormous reservoirs of biodiversity. The vast sprawl of the so-called Inland Empire and the city of San Bernadino lie at their feet, and the great Mojave Desert begins on their northern side.

The San Bernadinos and the neighboring San Gabriels are high barriers that block moisture flowing in from the Pacific Ocean. Annual rainfall in the San Gabriel valley averages around forty centimeters (sixteen inches), with much yearly variation. In the mountains just a couple of kilometers and two thousand vertical meters away, it is nearly twice that amount. Some of the heaviest rainfall per hour that I've ever experienced has been in Pasadena.

Farther west, the Hollywood Hills are well known as the site of the Hollywood Sign (originally erected as a real estate developer's advertisement). But geologically, the hills are the eastern tip of the sixty-kilometer range known as the Santa Monica Mountains that ends far north of Los Angeles at Point Mugu in Ventura County. An extension continues under the Pacific Ocean, then reemerges more than forty kilometers offshore as the Channel Islands. The Hollywood Hills also serve to separate the San Fernando Valley to the north from the Los Angeles basin to the south. The Santa Monicas are rugged and still wild in some places, but overall more modest in scale than either the San Gabriels or San Bernadinos. And as a coastal range, their western and southern flanks are in a climate zone that is very different from those of neighboring ranges. Hot summer months here are never as hot as elsewhere in the region, with the coastal air moderating the intense heat.

Botanically, the three ranges are very different, both from one another and from the plains below. The San Gabriels and San

Bernadinos are sky islands, isolated high-elevation ecosystems with animal and plant inhabitants distinct from those not far away. In the uppermost reaches above 2,000 meters of elevation, lodgepole, Jeffrey, and sugar pines dominate. Lower on the mountain slope, the pines meld into a lovely woodland of oak, maple, sycamore, and cottonwood: towering deciduous trees bowering over flowing streams in canyon troughs. Still lower, the foothills and lowlands are dotted with oaks, manzanitas, and sages. Rocky arroyos paved with granite boulders brim with mountain runoff in winter, and run dry in summer. The Santa Monicas, with their lower elevation and more coastal climate feature a somewhat different range of plant communities that includes oak savanna—the remnants of great plains of valley oaks (Quercus lobata) that once dominated Central and Southern California.

The canyons of Los Angeles are repositories of our biodiversity. Their rugged terrain meant that they were invaded last by the real estate developers. By the time the developers had parceled out the flatlands into urban and suburban housing subdivisions, at least some of the canyons had been given legal protection from builders. Some, like Glen Canyon and its trendy Beverly Hills neighborhood or Laurel Canyon and its iconic historical musical landmarks, are today known for both their natural and cultural features. Along with the beaches, they are the lungs of the basin. From Santa Anita Canyon in the east, to Runyon in the Hollywood Hills, to Malibu Canyon running down to the sea, the streambeds that cut through the mountain ranges are full of natural beauty and historic neighborhoods.

This topography is key to understanding the flora and fauna of the Los Angeles basin. The mountain ranges encircle and frame the basin's climate, and its plant and animal life. For better and worse, what happens in the basin tends to stay in the basin. The basin itself, ten thousand square kilometers of coastal plain—ancient sediment that was once the ocean floor—spreads from the foothills, across river drainages to the coast. Pools of natural asphalt, the so-called Tar Pits, occur in a few locales, and deep underground lie myriad seismic fault lines that occasionally wake up and terrify all Angelenos.

During my first weeks in Los Angeles in the 1990s, I botanized from my car as I drove the freeways. Swaying palm trees, icons of the Los Angeles landscape, studded the expanse of blue sky. The tallest, elegantly bowed palms were native to Australia and South America. The stately verdant palms with their clusters of amber fruits were from the Canary Islands. Even the ubiquitous fan palms were not the species native to the Los Angeles basin, but rather to Baja California.

The Los Angeles basin is a jigsaw puzzle of an ecosystem, with ever new forms of plant and animal interactions that deserve our attention. That word *interaction* is all-important. In a natural ecosystem, nearly every component is interlocked with other components. Pull one out and some aspect of the ecosystem may collapse. In our anthropogenic Southern California ecosystem, where the plants and animals didn't necessarily evolve with each other and many weren't even meant to live in this climate, that's not the case. We will explore this intricate web of relationships among creatures and plants from all parts of the globe that have been transplanted, and how they manage to coexist.

It matters enormously whether your neighborhood is full of local oaks and sages, or exotic palms, roses, and green lawns. Many flowering plants in our suburbs feed hummingbirds and butterflies, giving us the illusion that they're perfect proxies for the flowering plants that belong here. But they're really not good surrogates, because exotic plants tend to feed only those native creatures that can cope with a wide range of food sources. Generalists thrive and specialists die in a human-altered landscape; that is the rule. And there are far more habitat specialists out there than habitat generalists. House finches, squirrels and raccoons, and invasive grasses take over. The myriad other species that need a particular plant or prey animal to carry out their lives die out, only to be replaced by more hardy, adaptable survivors.

Most locals consider the plants and animals around them to be indigenous, or else couldn't care less where they originated. Nonnatives that beautify the surroundings are accepted, even beloved. Those that create havoc are eventually reviled, although often only by cities or homeowners that have to spend money and time to deal with them. Palms are iconic of life in LA and beloved until their fronds fall onto your new car. Raccoons are adorable until they're fighting with your dog and knocking over your trash cans every night. Coyotes howling in your local canyon are a wonderful reminder of how close we are to wild Nature in Los Angeles, until they carry away your cat.

Most Angelenos are oblivious to the environmental havoc of suburbia; in fact, most like it. I wrote this book to chart how thoroughly transformed the suburban world is from the native landscape, and to explore the lives and interactions of animals and plants that live here. In the following twenty-six chapters, I highlight species that one might encounter on a walk through a suburban neighborhood or our local hills. Our feelings and perceptions of the life around us run the gamut from admiration to ignorance to loathing, and I've tried to capture those perceptions in arranging this book.

We begin with the "stars of the suburbs," plants and animals iconic to all who live here. In later sections I've chosen to include species or groups that are equally important to ecologists, but often overlooked or even disdained by residents. In almost every case they're species that interact with us in some way. Some have vocal constituencies of fans and detractors. Some make do with an ecosystem utterly alien to their ancestors. Others are not so adaptable and cannot cope with the myriad nonnative plants and animals and human detritus around them. Some rely on foods that are nutritious but wildly unnatural. Others eke out a living on the scant remaining natural resources in our suburbs. Native or invasive, thriving or disappearing, they are united as part of the fabric of this strange ecosystem we call Los Angeles.

I.

STARS OF SUBURBIA

1

Palms Up,
and Down

Starting in the 1960s, every fourth grader in a California public school was required to do a mission project as part of learning the state's history. It was a celebration of the twenty-one religious out-posts established by the colonial Spanish government and the missionary Junipero Serra in the mid-eighteenth century, centers of enslavement and torture for tens of thousands of Indigenous people (the requirement was dropped when the history of the missions' oppression of Indigenous peoples was fully realized by historians). Many of the missions grew into towns and cities: San Diego, Santa Barbara, San Jose. Each child chose a mission and built a model of it to share with the class. Cardboard, popsicle sticks, and glued sugar cubes were the usual building materials. When my daughter's time came, I made a pilgrimage to the local crafts store to buy supplies to make our local San Gabriel mission. I explained my project to the salesman, who had likely heard this story a thousand times, and showed him my list of items. The savvy salesman scanned the list and stopped at palm trees. Eyebrows raised, he asked me sardonically just why I wanted a palm tree in my mission. I knew he had me, but I wasn't sure why. "What makes you think there were palm trees in the early history of Los Angeles?" he asked accusingly. I surrendered to his advice and made tiny fake oak trees instead.

My salesman-cum-historian was referencing the fact that the iconic palms of the Los Angeles landscape—except for one rarely planted variety— are recent imports to our human-altered ecosystem. Along the gritty industrial freeways, the broad boulevards of Beverly Hills, and the winding wooded streets of the Hollywood Hills, you'll see palm trees. In Beechwood Canyon, the neighborhood just below the Hollywood Sign, tourists try their best to snap a photo for Instagram that features the sign in the background, framed by a palm or two in the foreground.

Palms are trees-but-not-trees. They are often tall with something that looks like a trunk, but actually are very distant relatives of those other large plants we call trees. The "trunk" of a palm is not woody; it's more like an extraordinarily strong cable of woven fibers. This adaptation allows palms to bend without breaking in the strong coastal storms that impact many plant species. Their root systems are typically far shallower than those of trees, which makes them easy to transplant even at large sizes, and contributes to their desirability in landscaping. Palms are angiosperms, part of the vast radiation of flowering plants that emerged fifty-plus million years ago and came to dominate a botanic world that until that time had been populated

by non-flowering ferns, cycads, and coniferous trees. They are monocots; their seeds usually contain only one embryonic leaf cover, or cotyledon. Palms,
grasses, grains, bamboos, and many tropical plants are all
monocots.

Palms became the iconic trees of Southern California
because they symbolize an exotic haven in an arid place: an
oasis. You're trudging across a furnace-hot stretch of desert
landscape and spy a distant clump of palms. They indicate
water, either at the surface or just below it. As you approach,
the unrelenting heat of the desert is relieved by deep shade
under the clustered crowns of the palms. The fronds rus-
tle in a slight breeze. Even though there's no standing surface water,
buzzing of bees and patches of damp earth are telltale signs of water
beneath. If you search carefully, you'll likely find a trickle of water
coming from a hidden spring.

Because of their mutual dependence on water, palms and human
settlements are often neighbors. The chain of mission settlements in
California was built around reliable water sources. The California fan

palm (*Washingtonia filifera*), our only native palm, might have already been growing at some of the southern mission locales before the missions were built. Fan palms were likely planted as ornamental trees starting around the same time, probably by Spanish missionaries.

The depression years of the 1930s were the heyday of palm planting here in Los Angeles. Cities, including my own Pasadena, planted them everywhere as landscape trees, sometimes to provide work for the legions of unemployed laborers of that era. Some of these nearly century-old palms are still standing. By some estimates, as many as one hundred thousand palms of several varieties had been planted in the Los Angeles basin by the late twentieth century.

Palms had long been associated with tropical places like the South Pacific and the Caribbean, marketed as vacation destinations. As palms became symbols of LA, they helped market Southern California as a paradisical place to live in. A palm is perhaps the least utilitarian tree imaginable. Oaks, sycamores, maples, and the like provide abundant shade, and their roots prevent erosion. Palms do neither of these. But they evoke a vision of Los Angeles that has attracted newcomers and tourists for generations.

There are about four thousand species of palms worldwide, but only a handful are planted widely here. The native California fan palm grows near oases, springs, and seasonally wet arroyos in the Sonoran, Colorado, and Mojave deserts of the southeastern part of the state, and also in northernmost Baja California. Despite being the indigenous Los Angeles palm and so a natural part of our landscape, this is not the species of *Washingtonia* most often planted. The Mexican fan palm (*Washingtonia robusta*) is the most widely planted palm in the basin, standing above the industrial sprawl and lining the freeways of LA. It grows fast and handles freezing snaps well. Taller, straighter, and sturdier than the native California fan palm, it has the more iconic, spindly palm look favored by Southern California landscaping, though lacks the archetypal beauty of palms from more tropical locales, topped with only a relatively small crown of fronds. Because the old, dead fronds fold down onto the "trunk" instead of falling off, city workers spend weeks every year trimming the fibrous skirts to prevent falling fronds and to discourage rats from nesting therein.

The Mexican fan palm is planted ornamentally across the warmer parts of the southern United States, as far north in California as the San Francisco Bay Area, and around the Mediterranean, but it's native to the northwestern Mexican states of Sonora and Baja California. It may be slightly less cold tolerant than its California fan palm relative. In the Los Angeles basin, many palms appear to be hybrids of the two species, created either intentionally by arborists or accidentally when the species were growing near each other. Although it might seem odd to consider a palm an invasive species, the Mexican fan palm fits the description, so tough and growing so rapidly that it establishes itself in places in Southern California where no palms should grow, along streams and in moist canyon bottoms, potentially displacing native trees.

While the Mexican and California fan palms are the most iconic of all Los Angeles plants, several other palms are widely planted too. Some, like the famed coconut palm *(Cocos nucifera)* of the tropical South Pacific are too cold sensitive to survive in Southern California's temperate seasonal climate. Having coconuts that fall on pedestrians and cars wouldn't win the species any local fans either. Other palms have, however, prospered here. My own favorite is the Canary Island date palm *(Phoenix canariensis)*. Native to the Canary Islands off the coast of North Africa, it features a strongly ringed trunk and bunches of bright orange fruits that, combined with a wide crown of long, dark green fronds, are a spectacular landscape feature. Canary Island date palms line some of the stateliest boulevards in Los Angeles, and provide striking visual brackets to the entrance to many hotels, estates, stadiums, Disneyland, and the like. Compared to other palms planted here, Canary Island date palms grow slowly, only a few inches per year, making them valuable commodities in the commercial landscaping industry. Palm landscapers peruse neighborhoods looking for date palms in yards, then offer trivial amounts of money to remove them for unsuspecting homeowners, who see them only as pests whose roots threaten to invade their sewer pipes. But extracted from a lawn and pruned artfully, the tree can be resold for thousands of dollars.

The king palm *(Archontophoenix cunninghamiana,* or sometimes a related species, *A. alexander)* is a graceful, arching, forty-foot species native to the moist, warm eastern coast of Australia. It has a graceful coconut palm-ish appearance, the silver undersides of its fronds providing contrast from their green upper surfaces. Long draping bunches of red fruit hang just below the crown. It's a lovely tree, although somewhat limited in landscaping by its vulnerability to cold snaps and therefore more common in Southern California than farther north. The king palm is ironically a threatened species in its native Australia, but a widely planted ornamental in Southern California and even considered an invasive weed species in Brazil and elsewhere.

Gardening enthusiasts in Southern California often speak of king and queen palms in the same breath, but they have little connection to one another. The beautiful queen palm *(Syagrus romanzoffiana)* is a somewhat smaller species, reaching perhaps forty feet and topped with gracefully droopy, exceptionally long fronds and bright orange fruits. They are found naturally across a wide swath of South

America, usually in moist riverside areas, and are planted in warm regions all over the world, including the Los Angeles basin. But their thirsty nature means they're poorly suited to a drought-stricken climate, and they suffer in cold snaps too.

The trees above are the most commonly planted palms in the Los Angeles basin, though hardly the only ones. The Chilean wine palm (*Jubaea chilensis*), for instance, is increasingly planted, especially in place of dying palms of the more common species. Native to its eponymous Chile, it's a thick-trunked tree that at first glance resembles a Canary Island date palm. A mature specimen is equally magnificent. The species, being native to drier climes with some elevation, is very tolerant of aridity and cold temperatures that would eventually kill other palms. The Chilean wine palm's main liability as a landscape tree is its extremely slow growth rate. The statuesque, tall, thick-trunked specimens that are most valued in landscaping are decades old, so they don't serve well as replacements for fallen or dead palms unless they are transplanted as adults, which is an expensive undertaking.

In recent years, palms have lost their luster in a more water-wise and climate change–impacted California. Palms are thirsty trees, adapted to growing around oases but not ideally suited to a region that experiences periodic droughts. They are also prone to insect pest attacks and fungal infections. That, combined with the tendency of palms to drop their heavy fronds onto streets, cars, and pedestrians, forces cities to invest time and money to keep them healthy and trimmed. The *Washingtonia* palms' thick collar of thatch under the crown is beloved habitat for rats, which in the absence of a winter freeze find Los Angeles a lovely year-round environment to infest. And, of course, palms provide little shade compared to trees with spreading crowns.

These factors, but particularly their need for water, have fed a movement to remove palms from Southern California cities, or at least to replace them with drought-adapted trees after they die. Homeowners, seduced by a vision of a swaying palm over a backyard pool, find them obnoxiously difficult and expensive to maintain. The thousands of palms planted in the 1930s are old now, and susceptible to myriad pests and health issues. The South American palm weevil arrived in the United States in the past decade and has now made it to the Los Angeles area, killing hundreds of Canary Island date palms. A fungus called *Fusarium* has also been a major killer of Canary Island date palms. This species will likely be the first to disappear from the Los Angeles landscape, because of its susceptibility to a variety of insect pests and fatal infections caused by unclean pruning tools.

Cities have, for the most part, stopped planting palms. Many cities are trying to restore the native oak populations that once covered the region and have suffered tremendously from suburbanization. These majestic oaks, rapidly disappearing from our landscape, belong here. The palms do not.

Los Angeles has decreed that some palm stands will be preserved or replanted because they are iconic to the character of the region. The Elysian Park area around Dodger Stadium and nearby Echo Lake Park have already lost many of their palms. Chilean wine palms are being planted to replace them, although it will be decades before the new palms have matured enough to restore the postcard-from-LA look of those places. Some developers will no doubt still plant them to attract naive home buyers from outside Southern California who still see the palm as a magical property feature and don't realize how much water they guzzle.

In the 1990s, there were an estimated one hundred thousand palm trees in the Los Angeles basin. There are fewer today, and will be far fewer in the future. Palm trees may forever be iconic of Los Angeles glamor, but in a twenty-first century that is hotter, drier, and more prone to fires, we are slowly saying goodbye to them as we are to many nonnative plants, and good riddance. Let's hope they will be replaced by natives that feed the other parts of our unique ecosystem.

2

Winged Gemstones

My backyard in late afternoon sounds like an airport for tiny planes, with constant buzzing, strafing, and aerial dogfights. It's the hummingbirds getting their last chance at a carb-rich meal of sucrose before settling down for the night. The yard is planted to attract and feed them, with California lilacs *(Ceanothus spp.)*, sages *(Salvia spp.)*, and a number of hanging feeders filled with sugar water.

Hummingbirds, those tiny, buzzy-winged jewels, are fairly rare sights in most of eastern North America. But in the Southwest they're everywhere, with a diversity of species that is the result of proximity to their roots in Latin America. In the United States, southeastern Arizona is the epicenter of hummingbirds. Mexican species follow sky island mountains across the border into the US. Feeders there attract gigantic (a relative label in the hummingbird world) rainbow-hued hummers like the magnificent and blue-throated species. There are about three hundred fifty hummingbird species, and more than thirty species in North America alone, some of which occasionally stray across our southwestern border or waft over from the Caribbean into southern Florida. Of these, six species occur in or visit Los Angeles suburbs, and three of them call Los Angeles a year-round home.

Hummingbirds are widespread and successful in the Western Hemisphere, reaching their peak diversity in Central and South America, with a fraction of the group reaching North America. One species, the bronzy rufous hummingbird, is found all the way to Alaska in summer, and frequents the highest alpine flower meadows of western North America. In Africa and Asia, sunbirds are the size of hummers and also brilliantly feathered, but they flit from flower to flower more like a conventional bird instead of zooming forward and backward and hovering. Fascinating that half a world apart, Africa and Asia both spawned little nectar-feeding birds that look like flying jewels. Sunbirds are only distantly related to hummingbirds; their closest kin are actually crows and jays, while hummers are closer to swifts. Biologists call this suite of similarities between unrelated creatures convergent evolution, but the reason behind the iridescent color parallel is not entirely clear. We believe the earliest hummingbird ancestors split from swifts in Eurasia tens of millions of years ago, making their way over the Siberian land bridge into North America, and eventually south into the tropics, where they radiated into the several lineages and dozens of species they currently represent.

Hummingbirds are unique among birds in a variety of ways. Their ability to hover and to fly backward, like many insects, sets them apart from all other living vertebrates. Their wings beat dozens of times per second, not just up and down but in figure eights. Their bizarre feeding anatomy and technique employ a tongue so long that it wraps up inside the bird's tiny skull, the end split to form adjacent tubes that draw nectar upward toward the mouth. We long believed their method of drinking nectar to be capillary action, but we now know that their side-by-side tongue tubes flick in and out of flowers many times per second. As a bird feeds from a flower, its saber-like bill squeezes the tongue tubes flat together at their tips. When these tips open slightly, nectar rushes in. And as their tongue refurls itself, the tubes roll themselves back up, capturing the nectar and trapping it, an elegantly complex way of obtaining a mouthful of calories. Most people don't realize that animal protein in the form of insects is also a part of a hummingbird's diet. I've seen hummingbirds hover above my compost bin, snapping up fruit flies left and right.

Watching a hummingbird forage for nectar in your backyard doesn't give you a true appreciation of their amazingly precise foraging strategy. For that, you need to watch them forage in a large meadow of wildflowers, making successive passes up and down imaginary rows, pausing for a few seconds at each flower. The time he spends at each flower and the route he takes up and down and across the meadow are determined by finely tuned evolutionary tinkering to ensure he gets his sucrose. The optimal time spent at a flower should reflect the amount of nectar/calories reaped, relative to the amount of nectar he expects to obtain if he moves on a few seconds sooner or later. The route itself ought to be designed to maximize calories in while minimizing calories out. Hummingbirds have a relatively large brain-to-body ratio, suggesting intelligence. And scientists have long known that when it comes to foraging decisions, hummingbirds do indeed practice a strategy of optimizing their nutrient intake. It shouldn't be surprising at all, given the frenetic pace at which these tiny birds live their lives.

Hummingbirds are the gems of many Los Angeles backyards. At least four species visit my flowers and feeders, two of them daily and the other two seasonally. All are beautiful, especially adult males in breeding colors. The most abundant species, the Allen's hummingbird (*Selasphorus sasin*), rules the roost and the sugar-water feeders. Males show off a shimmering green back, usually with traces of rust-orange on the tail, and a bib (called a gorget) of ruby red.

Allen's hummingbirds are three inches of pugnacity. My several feeders are hung twenty feet apart to try to prevent a single male from monopolizing the whole sugar supply, but they still try to. Their animated buzzing fills the yard. Their tail feathers even contribute to their noisemaking, emanating a clicking sound during flight. January is peak mating season here, and a male Allen's hummingbird stakes out his territory and sits in exposed, high tree branches to survey his kingdom and drive away intruders. His courtship flight is a frantic parabolic path in front of a female, preceding a dramatic deep dive, at the nadir of which he produces a fluttery courtship sound with his tail feathers. Other species have their distinctive signature tail feather flutter sounds.

The Allen's hummingbird is unusual in having some populations that don't migrate. These non-migratory groups have even been labeled as a separate subspecies, *S. s. sedentarius*, once confined only to the Channel Islands off the coast of Los Angeles, but in recent decades spreading across the twenty-six-mile-wide channel into backyards up and down the coast, likely abetted by exotic trees and flowering gardens and hummingbird feeders. It is one of the lucky birds that has adapted and thrived in a suburban setting, while many others have disappeared.

It's impossible to imagine a hummingbird as stately as the Anna's hummingbird (*Calypte anna*) going about its business among Allen's hummers. Aptly named for a French noble lady during the Napoleonic era, Anna's don't zig and zag like Allen's while feeding; instead, they are downright placid. They're rarely seen driving away other hummers from a feeder or a flowering plant, and their movements are slower, more direct, and more predictable. It's not that they're submissive to Allen's; they just aren't flustered by them and don't seem much to care about them. In appearance Anna's hummers look very similar to Allen's at first glance, but are actually quite different, with an emerald mantle and long wings that don't quite reach the end of the tail. Males possess a deep rose-red throat gorget and a pale breast. They're medium sized among the plethora of North American hummingbirds, and the largest of the species that frequents a Southern California garden.

Anna's hummingbirds are suburban success stories, perhaps even more so than Allen's. This is no small part due to their catholic nectar preferences. They drink happily from a wide variety of plants, from Australian bottlebrushes and blooming eucalyptus to the whole array of native plants. This has allowed them to expand their natural, pre-suburban distribution as much as any hummingbird worldwide. Anna's hummers don't really migrate, although some move up and down mountain slopes from summer to winter.

My favorite local hummingbird is the rufous (*Selasphorus rufus*). A male rufous hummingbird in full-on breeding plumage is a stunning sight, colored head to tail in iridescent bronze. He looks dipped in molten metal. There is usually a hint of green in his wings and a few green feathers flecking his deep-orange back. Like their very close relatives the Allen's hummers, rufous hummers are pugnacious little birds, driving other hummers away from feeders. I've also seen them dive-bombing orioles and squirrels that venture too near their food supply. Rufous hummingbirds are renowned for making perhaps the longest migratory flights of any animal of their diminutive size. They fly annually from Mexico to Alaska, and a few months later back again, a trip of some six thousand kilometers. They stop in our Los Angeles gardens to replenish their caloric supply before heading up or down the West Coast. If you see a hummingbird in Alaska, it's a rufous hummer. They also occupy alpine meadows high in the Sierra Nevada during the fleeting summers those meadows experience.

For hummingbird aficionados in Southern California suburbia, distinguishing rufous hummingbirds from Allen's hummingbirds can be confusing. During spring and fall migrations, both species can be common at backyard gardens and feeders, and they look so much alike that identifying them is difficult to impossible. To make matters more complicated, they hybridize freely. Their polygynous mating system—one male attempting to have multiple mates—may contribute to the prevalence of hybrids. This makes naming the species sitting at your feeder a moot point. Although rufous males have the brilliant cape of bronze while Allen's are greener with orange-brown patches, most male rufous have some green feathers and some male Allen's have substantial bronzy-orange in their feathers (although any "rufous" with substantial green is more likely an Allen's or a hybrid). Females and juveniles of the two species are essentially impossible to tell apart at a distance; both have greenish backs. The only tried and true way to distinguish them from a few feet away is by the shapes of their outermost tail feathers. The two most lateral tail feathers of an Allen's hummer are very thin, almost to the point of being thread-like. Those of the rufous are wider, like the rest of their tail feathers but smaller.

You might be wondering how in the world anyone can see the tiniest tail feathers of a hummingbird well enough to make this distinction. You'd be right that it's quite a feat, although the males often fan their tails as they alight at a feeder, especially if they're driving another hummer away. With a pair of binoculars—or even sometimes with the naked eye—it's possible to catch a glimpse of a hummer's outer tail feathers and identify the species. Hybrids between Allen's and rufous presumably show an intermediate form of tail feathers.

These three species of hummingbird account for the vast majority of hummer sightings in our backyards. But other species do show up, and if you have a sharp eye, you may spot them. Black-chinned hummingbirds (*Archilochus alexandri*) have a lovely, clean, white lower throat and a black chin, separated by a band of iridescent purple. They're not the most gaudily colored hummers, but they're among the most successful, with a wide geographic distribution across the western United States. I have them at my feeders for a few weeks each spring. Compared to Anna's hummingbirds, the black-chinned are smaller and quieter. Compared to the hyperactive Allen's and rufous, they are positively sedate.

Costa's hummingbirds (*Calypte costae*) are close relatives of Anna's, and like the Allen's-rufous relationship, may hybridize with their larger Anna's cousins. Their most noteworthy feature is their stunning wide gorget that reaches out at the corners like an iridescent handlebar moustache. They're residents of arid scrubby regions of the Southwest, usually in areas of cactus and ocotillo but also extending into Southern California backyards. I've never seen one here, although I've seen them often in Arizona and elsewhere.

The rarest hummingbird sighting likely to happen in a garden in suburban Los Angeles is also the tiniest. The calliope hummingbird (*Stellula calliope*) is three grams of frenetic energy. The male has a gorget composed of shining pink-red feathers on a white background, giving him a striped-necked appearance. Along with his diminutive size and stubby tail, he's distinctively bright green; females and immatures are drabber. Calliopes deploy their energy during their long migrations, traveling nearly ten thousand kilometers each way between the mountains of northwestern North America and their wintering grounds in Mexico. They appear in Southern California mainly during spring and fall migration.

Feeders have changed the lives of many bird species, but perhaps none more than those of hummingbirds. Suburbanites plant lots of flowers, some of which are useful for hummers. But a single feeder can provide the sucrose-rich fluids of more than a thousand flowers, and has the power to draw in hummers near and far. Many a homeowner who has grown accustomed to seeing a hummingbird or two in their backyard every day has hung out a feeder and watched the local population explode to dozens of birds calling on their yard at mealtime. Beyond that, feeders may persuade them to stay rather than migrate, although this is much debated among bird experts. During lean season when flowers are less available, the feeder more than replaces natural nectar sources. In all likelihood, feeding hummingbirds all year round in Southern California is fine, since there are always alternative food plants available as well. In more northern latitudes, feeding them may cause them to linger until cold weather sets in, preventing them from surviving their eventual migration.

The abundance and diversity of hummingbirds in our gardens is not without controversy. Each sugar-water feeder represents a super-abundant source of nutrients, a gigantic windfall that causes the birds to make your yard a preferred hangout and perhaps even an essential food source. The sucrose, once ingested, is quickly converted to body fat the bird needs, especially during migration. Most homeowners use a sugar and water solution in a ratio of one to four, or 20 percent sucrose. Flowers, by comparison, offer a somewhat higher sucrose concentration and are gram for gram a better energy source for hummers. The shape and size of the feeder doesn't really matter; people in less affluent countries than the United States use all manner of discarded household objects to store sugar water with great hummer-attracting success. I have both hanging bottles and hanging plastic pans; the pans are less attractive but seem more popular. They also attract other bird species that hope to glean a bit of sweetener. Orioles are able to fit their longish slender bills partway into the feeding holes of the pan feeders. The feeders also attract hordes of ants and honeybees.

If setting out feeders full of the sucrose that hummingbirds so desperately seek is overtly unnatural, other less obvious interferences with the natural order may come into play too. Some of the food plants heralded as sure-fire hummingbird (and butterfly) attractants may have negative environmental impacts. The popular butterfly plant (Buddleia davidii) is a wonderful food plant for a variety of our backyard visitors, including hummers and butterflies, but it is not a host plant for caterpillars, limiting its usefulness for our native insect diversity. It is also an invasive species and can spread into local canyons and fields, crowding out native plants.

Hummingbirds are one of the greatest wildlife blessings of living in suburban Southern California. Moreover, they play an essential role as pollinators in a Southern California landscape. It would be a shame to become jaded about these little gems, because if an intergalactic biologist visited Earth, these would be among her most prized discoveries. From their beauty to their bizarrely wonderful anatomy, they are a tiny but spectacular part of our local ecology.

3

Painted Beauties among the Flowers

They come every year. Their black-framed tangerine wings flit from milkweed to milkweed, alighting just for a moment to sip some nectar or quickly deposit an egg or two on the underside of a leaf. A few weeks later, the milkweed leaves sag under the weight of fat, multicolored caterpillars, happily munching their way toward the day when they form lime-green chrysalises, then emerge as soggy-winged, bright-orange adults. A few hours drying out in the air and a new monarch is ready to join their species' migrations up and down the continent. Anyone who doesn't appreciate a monarch in the garden doesn't appreciate Nature's beauty. They are, in the insect world, the pride and joy of all who love backyard wildlife.

As I noted in the introduction, many of the animals and plants that share the Los Angeles suburbs with us are generalists: thriving in many settings, eating a wide array of foods. Monarchs are the opposite. Their ancestors carved out a niche long ago by relying, both as adults and as larvae, on a single plant—milkweed—that is noxious to many other animals. Milkweed contains toxic chemical compounds and also exudes the milky sap that gives the plant its name, which is difficult for the mouthparts of most insects to handle. Monarch caterpillars have no such trouble, and literally live to eat a plant that few other species want to eat. This has served them well in their million years of coexistence, right up until the moment when suburban development and the industrial-scale spraying of pesticides caused milkweed populations across North America to crash, taking these beautiful butterflies along with them. Some genetically engineered crops are bred to withstand pesticides that wipe out all the other plant species around them, including the milkweeds, so the fallow areas of crop field no longer provide anything for monarchs except death.

Those who venture to monarchs' winter roosts in California, or to the spectacular ones in the mountains of central Mexico, stand among an orange snowfall of a hundred thousand fluttering monarchs. Yet this is the tiniest remnant of what was once a far more vast assemblage. The billion monarchs that flew across the Great Plains and into Mexico each fall were one of the largest mass migrations of any animal on Earth. Monarchs are now more than 90 percent reduced across their range, and 99.9 percent gone from California—from millions wintering in the state to now only a handful. Much of this devastation has happened just in the past decade. During the period from 2015 to 2020, the number of monarchs overwintering in California dropped to just two thousand butterflies. The following year showed an uptick in winter populations, to fifty thousand. But those numbers pale with those of the recent past. What has happened to monarchs is the insect equivalent of the great bison slaughter of the 1800s.

Monarchs are not the only spectacular butterflies to grace our backyards; more than one hundred butterfly species live in the Los Angeles area. I have loved swallowtails (genus *Papilio*) since growing up in the eastern United States, where they would flap into grapevines and apple trees in my neighborhood. We have a few stunningly beautiful swallowtails in the Los Angeles area. The anise swallowtail (*P. zelicaon*) is the most commonly seen. I've witnessed amazing gatherings of these butterflies on hilltops in the San Gabriel Mountains, where males and females go to find each other in spring. The adults are attracted to a variety of native plants, and also invasive plants like fennel, while the larvae eat their way through our leafy garden herbs and vegetables. The other common swallowtail is the striking western tiger swallowtail (*P. rutulus*), a big, showy butterfly that uses many of our local trees—like alders, wild cherries, and willows—for nectar, and whose larvae love the leaves of the same species. The even larger giant swallowtail (*P. cresphontes*) and the pale swallowtail (*P. eurymedon*) also occur in the LA basin.

None of LA's other butterflies can match the monarch and swallowtails for size and showiness, but our butterfly diversity is nonetheless impressive. From medium-sized fritillaries and metalmarks, to smallish ladies, to the little skippers and even tinier blues, dozens of species regularly appear in our gardens and parks. Some of these species are not even native. The lovely orange gulf fritillary (*Agraulis vanillae incarnata*) is a tropical butterfly that was introduced to the United States a century ago and thrives anywhere it can find its host plant, the passion vine. If you have some passion vine trailing along a fence in your backyard, gulf fritillaries are sure to show up. Some other little beauties like the cabbage white (*Pieris rapae*) and red admiral *(Vanessa atalanta)* occur across large swaths of the globe and are highly adaptable to many food plants. Painted ladies *(Vanessa cardui)*, possibly the world's most common and widespread butterflies, are released by the millions by schoolroom butterfly breeding projects. They migrate through our area, especially during rainy winters, traveling between the deserts of Mexico and the Pacific Northwest. Like monarchs and other butterfly species, painted ladies' migration is quite different from that of birds. These butterflies make the trip in multiple generations; an adult flies for days, lays eggs, and dies, and the offspring hatch out and once metamorphosed continue the migratory journey.

Of all the tiny butterflies that many garden owners don't notice fluttering around their flowers, the skippers are most visible. They crowd preferred food plants, and some of the most widely planted ornamentals are adult skippers' favored haunts. The fiery skipper *(Hylephila phyleus)* is common in Southern California, gracing lantanas and other nonnative landscaping plants with its mottled gold-orange and brown wings. Skippers look moth-like because they are: their family, Hesperiidae, is classified between butterfly and moth. They appear hairier than most butterflies, with very short, horn-like antennae.

When perched, they hold their wings up and closed, a distinctive identifying mark. The male's colors are more vivid than those of the pastel-shaded female. While they can live on introduced plants, their natural diet is our native buckwheat, yarrows, locusts, and legumes. Their larvae cope with suburbia well because they eat grass and weeds. The tiny caterpillars of some skippers create shelters for themselves in lawns by binding grass blades together.

As small as most skipper species are, the blues in particular achieve a level of diminutive beauty unparalleled in the butterfly world. They tend to go unnoticed unless they have been deprived of their host plants and habitat to such an extent that local naturalists call attention to their plight. In the Los Angeles basin, two species—actually local variants of more widespread species, or subspecies—are federally protected, and lost habitat has been restored to ensure their future. In El Segundo, just south of Los Angeles International Airport, a reserve is established for the protection of the El Segundo blue *(Euphilotes battoides allyni)*, a fluttering nymph with lavender-blue upperwings and pale-spotted underwings. Decades ago, the reserve was a trendy seaside town called Surfridge, and the skippers called the entire coastal strip their home. Then came the ever-expanding behemoth transit hub that is LAX. The town shuttered. Today, the remnants of palm-lined streets remain in the ghost town that is the El Segundo Blue Butterfly Preserve.

In summer, the El Segundo blue population briefly swells to the hundreds of thousands, all limited to their tiny patches of real estate. They survive entirely on the good graces of one host plant, the coast buckwheat *(Eriogonum parvifolium)*. Adults feed on its nectar while larvae hatch and develop on the plant before pupating in the sandy soil underneath, then metamorphosing to start the life cycle anew.

The El Segundo blue is only one of many blues in the Los Angeles basin, some of which are federally endangered while others are downright common. The acmon blue *(Icaricia acmon)* is widespread up and down the West Coast. Males are a stunning purply-blue with an orange band on their rear wings; females are cloaked in subtler pastels. Acmon blues also live on buckwheat plants but are more catholic in their tastes than El Segundo blues, and thus are not as habitat limited. The marine blue *(Leptotes marina)* is even more widespread and likely the most common of the many blue species in the western United States.

Just down the coastline from the El Segundo blue, the Palos Verdes blue (*Glaucopsyche lygdamus palosverdesensis*) was thought to be extinct only ten years after its discovery when its only known habitat was bulldozed in the 1980s. This left the species with only a few known surviving pairs until another population was discovered in 1994 in the San Pedro area. Conservationists began breeding them in captivity, and many hundreds of pupae were introduced to the wild. Since then, the total known population has remained in the low hundreds, in danger of a severe storm or wanton development wiping out the species. The Palos Verdes blue is one of the rarest butterflies in North America, if not the entire world.

In addition to the many species of blues, other Los Angeles butterflies abound. The lugubriously named funereal duskywing (*Erynnis funeralis*) is a mostly dark-colored frequent visitor to the sunflowers and buckwheat in my yard, and the very similar mournful duskywing (*Erynnis tristis*) is an oak specialist that flits along the oak-lined canyon at the end of my street.

The metalmarks (genera *Apodemia* and *Calephelis*) are diminutive butterflies, most of them with metallic-looking marks on their wings. They use a variety of native California buckwheats and sunflowers as food and larval host plants, and are fairly common in our area if one searches in the right places. The checkerspots (genus *Euphydryas*) are likewise fairly common, and one—the variable checkerspot (*E. chalcedona*)—is downright abundant in spring. Among the hairstreaks, the lovely gray hairstreak (*Strymon melinus*) is also a common species in the LA basin, another generalist when it comes to diet and host plants. Native habitat may be scarcer than in the past, but local gardens and weedy urban lots can provide for its needs.

The mere sight of fluttering butterflies in a garden sends most people into lyrical moods about the beauty of Nature, when the sterile green lawns surrounding that garden have nothing to attract those butterflies. We've come to take their general absence for granted and spend our energy and money on unnatural and even artificial decorations in place of them. A simple gathering of beautiful insects reminds us what has been lost, how much the baseline has slipped.

The bottom line when it comes to butterflies in our Los Angeles ecosystem is that they cannot be considered separately from their caterpillar larvae, nor from the flowers that feed them. This is where the native versus nonnative dichotomy matters. I'm not a fan of purity tests when it comes to gardening. A garden that is partly but not entirely made up of natives is nevertheless a huge boon to the biodiversity of the Los Angeles basin. In fact, even if a minority of plants are native, that's still a major improvement over the ornamental garden status quo. But preserving butterfly habitat is tricky because even though our yards may be planted with pretty flowers that provide nectar for adults, food species for the caterpillar larvae are equally important. Those butterflies fluttering around your backyard ornamental butterfly bush (*Buddleia davidii*) are well fed, but the plant provides nothing to feed the larvae that hatch from their eggs. So, planting for caterpillars is often more critical than planting for butterflies. Moreover, caterpillars are part of the energy flow of the garden, and writ large of the ecosystem. They move nutrients through their habitat in the same way that larger herbivores do. They do this with an enormous number and diversity of tiny bites, rather than a smaller number of larger ones.

Monarchs are the iconic endangered butterfly for most Americans, but there are many threatened species that aren't federally protected as endangered species. This is because until very recently, the courts and the US government did not consider insects eligible for listing. As of 2020, insects including butterflies can be listed, but the government does not yet consider them high enough of a priority to warrant federal protection. You have to wonder if by the time the authorities act, it will be too late. In fact, the agency charged with coming up with a protective management plan has estimated that the odds of monarchs surviving the coming few decades are very close to zero. Industrial agricultural corporations and the government itself have already written off this most iconic of all American insects.

In Southern California, threats to monarch survival appear to be less from pesticides and more from the loss of their food plants due to suburban development. This is a problem with a solution: we all should simply plant a few native milkweeds around our homes. Prioritizing Nature is in this case essential in the long-term struggle to balance wildlife habitat and economic development. Thus far, the cards have been stacked entirely against monarchs, and that's why the overwintering sites that held millions just decades ago now hold only thousands. If we can't save one of the most iconic and beloved butterflies, what does that say about our will and ability to save all the others?

4

Peafowl Rule
This Roost

All too often, there are peacocks scratching around my front yard. More properly, peafowl, since peacocks refer only to adult males with their stunning trains of tail feathers. Females, or peahens, and their chicks enjoy my yard too. I walk out my front door to see a large depression in the soil where I've just planted a native plant. Something or someone has dug a shallow basin there, pushing the plant and its roots out of the way. The evidence trail isn't hard to follow. Blue feathers shine like stranded exotic fish scattered about the dirt area. A peafowl family has taken some dust baths.

The first time I discovered the crime I was slightly impressed; I knew there were peafowl populations all over Los Angeles, but didn't expect them in my new neighborhood. This flock turned out to be at least ten birds, thinned occasionally by encounters with moving cars, coyotes, and malicious people, and enhanced more than once a year by new clutches of chicks. Because of our proximity to the local canyon, packs of coyotes venture into the streets at night. I soon learned that the peafowl are careful to roost in tall trees and on rooftops between dusk and dawn to stay out of harm's way, depositing a sizeable quantity of peafowl poop in the process.

There are several different peafowl populations in the suburbs of Los Angeles; each one has a different origin story with a similar theme. A wealthy businessman buys a large tract of land in the late 1800s or early 1990s and establishes a ranch estate, then decides it would be fitting to have regal birds like peacocks strutting around on it. He imports a flock of peafowl from India—their natural range covers almost the whole Indian subcontinent (much rarer species of peafowl occur elsewhere but those in Los Angeles are the common Indian peafowl *(Pavo cristatus)*—and they begin to produce lots of chicks. Later, the business mogul dies and his land is divided for sale as much smaller parcels. The land changes ownership, and the peacocks, having wandered off, remain where they choose, making a living by scratching for insects and berries and being fed by local people who find their exotic beauty well worth the price of endless peafowl poop and noise.

The origin story of the peafowl in the Pasadena area starts with Elias "Lucky" Baldwin, a flamboyant entrepreneur who, among other achievements, brought horse racing to the San Gabriel Valley, establishing the famed Santa Anita Park racetrack in 1907. Decades earlier, Baldwin had arrived in the area and purchased the land, then called Rancho Santa Anita, that now comprises much of the cities of Arcadia, Pasadena, and Sierra Madre. He turned Santa Anita into an estate with fruit orchards and livestock. He also brought in a few dozen peafowl.

Upon Baldwin's death, the property was divided among his heirs and sold as parcels. Even Los Angeles County benefited, acquiring more than a hundred acres to establish the Los Angeles Arboretum in Arcadia. To this day, the botanical garden and the neighborhood surrounding it are overrun with peafowl that are largely the descendants of Baldwin's birds. According to legend, Baldwin at some point gifted some of this peafowl progeny to a business associate on the Palos Verde Peninsula, bringing a population of the birds to an entirely different part of Los Angeles. They immediately became both a boon and bane to the locals, some of whom today embrace them and some of whom definitely don't. The peafowl advocates feed the birds, provide them places to roost, even incubate their eggs for them and allow them to roam their patios and homes.

Peafowl are nothing if not noisy. When I was a graduate student doing animal behavior research in South Asia, I lived in a tiny village in the Indian desert state of Rajasthan. It was a scenic farming landscape dotted with villages of stone-and-mud houses with thatched roofs. People were mostly farmers, and camels and buffalo shared our living space. There were peafowl everywhere. They perched on rooftops at dawn, awakening us with their insistent wailing calls, like roosters crowing as the harbingers of the new day. For the first few days this was enjoyably exotic. After that, not so much. But the locals, having grown up with their calls each morning, didn't even notice. Tourist sites all over India are crawling with peafowl. The Mughal emperors liked peacocks; for American tourists they provided local flavor. In Los Angeles suburbs, they roam the streets fearlessly like preening royals, their wailing call penetrating the quietest of living rooms. It's a call that, once heard, can't be forgotten, with a siren quality that's either appealing or awful, depending on one's distance from it and the time of day.

The problem with peafowl is not just their noise and their poop. When peacocks catch a glimpse of their reflection in the body paint of a car, they have been known to inflict expensive damage by pecking savagely at their perceived rival. Visitors to the neighborhood are sometimes warned not to park their cars on the street if they're freshly washed, lest they end up with chipped paint or a dimpled fender.

Peacocks are among the most dramatic manifestations on the planet of Darwin's principle of sexual selection. Males are ornately feathered to the max; when they strut and court they fan out a tail that is larger than the rest of their body. Females are drab brown without over-the-top feather adornments, not for camouflage while incubating eggs, as was once believed, but because they have no evolutionary pressure to be visually arresting. Contrary to the old idea that females are merely the demure recipients of male reproductive ambitions, their choosiness about mates is in fact the driving force behind male peacock beauty. By preferring the most elaborate visual display imaginable, they set up a system in which any genetic mutation that conferred longer and brighter feathers on a male to be favored. Over time, peacocks became more and more colorful with larger and larger tails, as those males that possessed the most stunning tails got the most sex with discriminating females. Lacking such pressure, females stayed smaller and more drably colored. Males aren't bigger to protect their brood against predators; their evolutionary advantage is entirely selfish, to be chosen over other males.

The effect of male ornamentation on female mating interest has been tested in a wide range of animals, including many birds in which males have ornate features compared to females. Species in which males are a bright color often display a hierarchy in which the very

brightest-colored males in a
flock have the highest mating
success. In a local population
of peafowl, one or two males
may garner the vast majority
of matings, and they are typically
the males with the most impressive
tails. Research by Jessica Yorzinski
found that peahens spend an inordi-
nate amount of time staring at peacocks, clearly checking them out
to ascertain who is the most desirable. Why females would prefer
brightly colored males is obvious; it takes good nutrition to maintain
a sheen of bright plumage, and it takes a genetically strong bird to
obtain all the food he needs to be well nourished.

Researchers Roslyn Dakin and Robert Montgomerie showed that
the degree of iridescence (and by implication, the sheer number) of
eyespots—more properly called ocelli—in a peacock's magnificent
train of fanned-out tail feathers largely determines how aroused a
peahen is by him. When the researchers covered all the ocelli, the
male's mating success dropped to zero. They concluded that the
iridescence of the eyespots is the single most important influence
on peacock mating success, the feature most eagerly observed by
females while courting.

You might wonder how, in the forests of India while hunted by
leopards and tigers, peacocks could have possibly evolved such oversized, heavy tails. Peacock tails are considered to be examples of "run-
away sexual selection," in which a trait that appears to be patently bad
for survival is perpetuated, even further exaggerated, because it benefits male mating success. There is even a theory called "the handi-
cap principle," first thought up by the Israeli biologist Amotz Zahavi,

which holds that larger peacock tails are fancied by females precisely because of how encumbered they are by them. Zahavi argued that animals like peacocks are "telling" females that they've managed to avoid being eaten by predators despite the disability of an oversized tail that limits their mobility, signaling the outstanding quality of the genes they must possess.

Whatever biological factors explain a peacock's tail, it is a sight to behold both for peahens and human observers. I very much doubt that human residents would consider tolerating a flock of drab, turkey-sized birds pooping on their sidewalks and screeching them awake at dawn. Nevertheless, these annoying qualities of the birds have led to conflicts with residents, and in some cases, wholesale peafowl-icide.

On the southwestern side of Los Angeles, in tony, suburban Rolling Hills Estates—home to hundreds of peacocks, peahens, and peachicks—carcasses of peafowl began turning up on city streets. As you would expect, peafowl sometimes fall prey to coyotes, where the only forensic evidence is a pile of brightly colored feathers. Uneaten peafowl carcasses meant that something else was going on. Bird die-offs do happen; we had dozens of dead crows on our street during the West Nile Virus outbreak years ago. In this case, dozens of peafowl, more than 10 percent of the local population, were found dead over a several-week period in close proximity to each other. Autopsies showed that at least some of the peafowl had been shot with pellet or BB guns, and by bow and arrow. Some had even been bludgeoned at close range. It was unclear whether the birds were being used for target practice or if there was something more premediated happening, but the frequency of death was suspicious.

Peafowl might be as nonnative as it gets in Los Angeles, and might be considered invasive too, but it's nevertheless a felony to intentionally kill wildlife, punishable by a hefty fine and, theoretically at least, jail time. A few home owners who were suspects in the peafowl deaths because of their vocal anti-peafowl comments sold their homes on the peninsula and moved away. The peafowl killings in Rolling Hills Estates by and large stopped at that point.

Some local communities trap the birds humanely and relocate them to ranches or less-populated properties outside the Los Angeles area, where owners actively want peafowl roaming their land. As I was writing this book, some residents of my adopted hometown of South Pasadena complained loudly enough about the peafowl in the Monterey Hills part of town that the city agreed to hire a removal specialist to relocate them. A census estimated a population of more than a hundred adults in the area, up from just a few dozen two years earlier. In my view, the peafowl problem pales by comparison to the public nuisances of barking dogs, blaring leaf blowers and lawn mowers, and partying neighbors. But since no one owns the peafowl, the pro-peafowl lobby group is far less effective.

In a landscape filled with exotics, peafowl might be the most emblematic of Los Angeles's wildlife glamor. Their sublime shimmer shocks out-of-town visitors and friends on social media. Peafowl don't belong strutting around a suburban street, but previous generations brought them here and we live with the consequences. There's something both wonderful and awful about having them in our daily Southern California lives.

5

Cats Great and Small

The mountain lion was sitting by the curb like some oversized lawn statue as the couple drove up a winding road in the Hollywood Hills. It was night, and they were on their way home. The car went around a bend and the headlights swept onto the cat. They stopped to gawk, and the lion sat casually, posing for a minute, before heading off into the brush. He was an adult male, weighing more than a hundred pounds. He could easily bring down a deer or a large dog, and here he was idling in an upscale suburb. The story made the news for a day or so. Not many weeks later, the same lion was seen on a front door surveillance camera calmly strolling the neighborhood. It was P-22 (as in, the 22nd puma to be radio-collared by local wildlife biologists), a venerable and venerated now twelve-year old adult male who called Griffith Park his home for most of that time.

Los Angeles is one of only two places on Earth where big cats roam free inside city limits (the other is Mumbai, India, with its leopards). The mountain lion, better known as the puma across a large part of the Americas, or cougar in parts of the American West, or panther in Florida, is one of the world's largest and most impressive cats. To share our neighborhoods with even a remnant few is a profound honor and privilege.

At the time of his eventual death in late 2022, euthanized after he'd been hit by a car and was reduced to preying on neighborhood dogs, P-22 was among the oldest lions recorded in the two decades of field research on Los Angeles's mountain lions (his father P-1, was a bit older). His barely eight-square-mile kingdom was hemmed in on three sides by some of the most heavily traveled freeways in North America. Photographer Steve Winter's iconic 2013 image of P-22 roaming in Griffith Park with the Hollywood Sign and LA's freeways in the background captured the urban lion experience. That a half million people daily rush past a forest in which a mountain lion lives is breathtaking in itself.

P-22's life story is remarkably well-known, and his death was widely memorialized by Angelenos, including the Tongva and other local tribes who related to this magnificent being displaced from his home by the sprawl of development. P-22 was a remarkable urban big cat in America's most media-obsessed city. He lived in and around Griffith Park since he was radio-collared in 2012 as young animal. Based on his genetic profile, he was likely born in the Santa Monica Mountains. This means that in order to reach Griffith Park earlier in his long life, he had to cross both the north and southbound lanes of the 101 and 405 Freeways, two of America's busiest. Even in the middle of the night, that's sixteen traffic lanes with cars and trucks traveling seventy-plus miles per hour. It's hard to contemplate doing that without being clobbered. Indeed, more than five hundred mountain lions died in roadkill accidents in California between 2015 and 2022, more than one per week; it's a leading cause of their decline across the state.

Mountain lions (*Puma concolor*) are apex predators; they normally range over areas of more than one hundred square miles in search of their favorite prey, mule deer, supplemented by raccoons and other smaller mammals. A mountain lion wearing a GPS tracking collar was observed to cross the Grand Canyon from rim to rim one day a few years ago. P-22 made do with a tiny fraction of a typical lion's territory, occupying what was probably the smallest territory of any wild mountain lion in the whole of their hemisphere-wide range from Alaska through Latin America. P-22 occasionally supplemented his diet by breaking into the highest-density animal spot in Griffith Park: the Los Angeles Zoo. Whether due to hunger or simply the joy of the hunt, he attacked and killed a few zoo animals over the span of his life, most notably an Australian koala.

The past couple of years have been bountiful for our local mountain lions, despite the deaths of at least two at the hands of cars on the freeways. A record number of kittens have been born. One of those litters was born to P-19, the oldest female in the study, who is believed to have birthed at least five litters in her ten years of life.

At least thirteen kittens were born in the Santa Monica Mountains in the summer of 2020 alone, in five litters to five different females. The total population of mountain lions in California is estimated at between three thousand and five thousand individuals, most of which live in the northern part of state. As of 2021, the Los Angeles basin is home to ten adults and subadults, with perhaps another one or two lions who pass through but are not wearing radio-collars and thus are not reported. While P-22's tiny home range was extreme in its smallness, even the lions that roam the Santa Monica Mountains to the west cope with hunting ranges that are likely smaller than those of lions in other more rural parts of the state.

Even if LA's mountain lions can survive freeway traffic, rat poison, and a lack of natural foods, they could be done in eventually by the loss of their genetic diversity. A 2018 study by Kyle Gustafson and colleagues found that the mountain lion populations of the state of California are sub-divided into at least nine genetically distinct sub-populations. Ongoing fragmentation of the lions' habitat serves to further fragment each population into smaller and more isolated genetic units. The populations can only cope with this for so long. Mountain lions are not a very genetically diverse species overall, the result of their near extinction back in the Pleistocene.

The North American mountain lion repopulated our region millennia ago when migrants from South America came north. The sub-populations of Los Angeles are small and already inbred. This trend will certainly increase in coming decades as urbanization spreads. This is in stark contrast to most mountain lion populations across the rural West, which tend to be highly diverse, due to the lions' tendency to range far and wide, and where there are few barriers to new in-and-out migration. Lions in the Sierra Nevada represent a large, genetically healthy population, partly because they are not hunted, and also because the original source population there was large and genetically diverse.

Starting in the 1980s, research by Paul Beier and colleagues established that Southern California mountain lions do what mountain lions do everywhere: they range far and wide in search of prey. Even back then, our local mountain ranges were rapidly becoming a refuge trapped between encircling freeways and suburbs. Male mountain lions normally search for mates and new hunting grounds, but our freeway system and vast suburban sprawl largely prevent that. The lions in and around the Los Angeles basin are mostly cut off from the much-needed migration of new lions from other areas. This will exacerbate inbreeding in the coming decades and spells major trouble for the long-term survival of lions in our region.

The Gustafson study showed that the mountain lions of our local San Gabriel and San Bernadino Mountain ranges are most similar genetically to those farther north, both on the coast and in the high Sierra. This suggests that our local lions live in an area of migration between several important populations, and that the survival of each population is key to preserving genetic connectivity and health of the whole region's lions. Preserving the wild lands in those regions is critically important.

Encountering a bobcat *(Lynx rufus)* on a trail might not be as breathtaking as meeting an ultra-rare mountain lion, but it's still exciting. Far more commonly seen than their larger feline kin, bobcats wander through many suburban neighborhoods, especially those that border on canyons and woodlands. Because of their small size (adults are fifteen to twenty pounds), they require a far smaller area for hunting, just a couple of square miles, and therefore turn up in places more urban than any mountain lion would. A bobcat was photographed by Los Angeles wildlife biologist Miguel Ordeñana on a nocturnal camera trap squeezing under a chain link fence in Elysian Park, a short walk from Dodger Stadium. A bobcat was recently recorded (in the form of a roadkill carcass) in trendy Silverlake, a very urban Los Angeles neighborhood. I have friends who have looked out their back door to see bobcats calmly lying on their backyard patio furniture like so many tabbies.

I've seen bobcats on a number of occasions in my life, usually on trails while hiking. When I see a tawny cat's head in the brush, my first hope is *mountain lion!*, and a millisecond later, I happily settle for *bobcat!* Once I was sitting in gridlocked car traffic leaving a popular hiking spot's parking area. As I stared out the window in abject boredom, a bobcat strolled calmly through the tall grass not ten feet from my car door. Between the two of us, I was the far more excited.

Bobcats are also fearsome suburban predators. They do well on the periphery of human activity because of the abundant supply of rats, mice, gophers, ground squirrels, and rabbits it provides them. They're small enough to hide in plain sight in and around backyards in the daytime, then come out to hunt at night. About once a week in my neighborhood, there's a social media post about bobcat sightings. Bobcats prowling streets at night; bobcats turning up outside the back door, the household kitty a few inches away behind the glass; bobcats caught on surveillance cameras lounging on patio furniture, napping by the swimming pool, gazing longingly at the family parrot in the window. A recent post on my neighborhood social media app bemoaned the death of the family rabbit at the hands of a local bobcat. The family had built a backyard enclosure that was seven feet tall but open on top, and one morning they found a bobcat tearing the bunny apart for its leisurely breakfast.

Humans admire their local wild cats, and bobcats aren't big enough to engender fear of harm, unless it's to the family cat or rabbit. They suffer, however, at human hands even while eking out a living among us. Being hit by cars and eating poison-laced rodents are two major causes of bobcat mortality in our area. And despite bobcats' far lesser spatial needs, they are vulnerable to the same harmful effects of genetic isolation that mountain lions suffer from. Biologists from the National Park Service and UCLA found that bobcats in the Santa Monica Mountains and the westernmost parts of the San Fernando Valley have suffered a loss of genetic diversity, much the same as mountain lions in our area. Genetic diversity is a protection against illness. Should an epidemic strike, the presence of many random genes increases the chances of at least some individuals developing immunity. These insular populations of bobcats and mountain lions lack the many random genes that might otherwise ensure their survival.

A team of researchers led by Laurel Serieys showed that the 101 and 405 Freeways are major barriers to migration for bobcats, just as they are to mountain lions, resulting in population fragmentation and ensuing loss of genetic diversity in the isolated subpopulations. The impact of the 405 Freeway was more sinister than that of the 101; migration across it was almost entirely from east to west. This may be because there is much less decent cat habitat to the east of the 405, and also because there are few crossing points over the 405 compared to the 101. As with mountain lions, the inbreeding that inevitably follows isolation leads to a greater eventual risk of local extinction.

In the end, the future of both mountain lions and bobcats in the Los Angeles basin and surrounding mountain ranges will come down to habitat connectivity. They are likely doomed unless corridors enable cats from one area to pass through to another to avoid mating with close relatives and replenish the local genetic diversity that has been lost over time. Even an occasional immigrant cat's genes—how occasional depends on the species and the context—can offset the harmful effects of inbreeding.

Wildlife corridors are gigantic investments in local biodiversity. They are metaphorically and literally bridges to a future Los Angeles landscape that, despite a rapidly burgeoning human population and intense demand for more living space, will include wild cats and other animals in that future. The wildlife corridor bridge currently under construction in Liberty Canyon near Malibu Creek State Park to span the 101 Freeway will be the world's largest (two hundred feet across a ten-lane freeway, and almost as wide as it will be long), the most urban, and the most costly at $90 million. The bridge, began in 2022, will be planted with native vegetation and traverse one of the most traveled roads on Earth, allowing mountains lions, bobcats, coyotes, mule deer, as well as a host of smaller animals, to move between the Santa Monica Mountains and the Simi Hills and other areas to the north. The corridor will not only facilitate animal migration within our area, but also between the Los Angeles basin and points much farther north. The lands on both sides of the corridor are state or county owned, and so this bridge could help the wildlife in perpetuity.

Given the vast maze of suburban development and eight-lane freeways that compose the Los Angeles basin, the conservation issues are complex. The cats' need to migrate both out of and into fragments of habitat clashes with development plans all across the Southland. The real estate market itself plays a role; land prices are already sky-high, and when they spike, it becomes that much more difficult for the city to set aside land for lions, bobcats, and other wildlife. We also need to understand how well corridors work in a given area before undertaking huge construction projects. Some corridors may need to be complete and well-wooded to serve their purpose; others may work well even if unplanted and incomplete. And in such a small population of lions, some individuals may be more willing to use corridors than others, which could make all the difference in preserving a genetically healthy population.

The enormous effort and expense of preserving a tiny population of Los Angeles mountain lions, and a larger population of bobcats, is rewarded by the preservation of some semblance of an ecosystem that functions for both cats and people. The cats benefit and the land benefits. Millions of residents cherish coexistence with such wildness. It's a shared responsibility, and a shared reward. The wildlife corridor and the overall conservation efforts are tributes to Angelenos for whom having wild cats roaming in their midst is as wonderful as any city dweller in the world can imagine.

6

The Spectacle

Every evening, a wildlife spectacle dazzles suburban Los Angeles. At various locations in the San Gabriel Valley, flocks of up to fifteen hundred large parrots fly home to their roosting trees. They've spent the day flying many miles across the basin in search of their favorite foods. Now the day is done and it's time for some intense socializing before bedding down for the night. The parrots clamber around the trees on otherwise quiet streets of a nondescript neighborhood, as raucous as parrots can be. They chatter, they squawk; they poop on your roof, your car, and pretty much everywhere else. Having a conversation while standing near the trees means shouting above the din. And don't even think of standing directly under a roosting tree.

Most residents would love the parrots gone. The roosting sites move around the valley from year to year, to the relief and chagrin of the various neighborhoods.

Neighborhood nuisance though they may be, the morning and evening flights of hundreds upon hundreds of large parrots across Los Angeles suburbia are simply spectacular, comparable to nothing else anywhere in North America. The nightly exodus of thousands of Mexican free-tailed bats from under the Congress Bridge in Austin, Texas, is the closest parallel. Globe-trotting ecotourists fly to tropical forests in Costa Rica to watch parrots fly overhead in huge flocks. Our parrots are literally above and around us, swarming the neighborhood.

In a landscape already divorced from its natural animals and plants, perhaps the parrots are charismatic fauna that we should embrace and celebrate. No parrots are native to the Los Angeles basin, but a sizeable population of several species are decidedly nonnative—nearly all from Latin America. An often-repeated urban legend recounts that the parrots of Los Angeles are descended from escapees from a pet store that burned down in the 1970s. In fact, our parrots almost certainly escaped or were released from captivity. Parrots were legally imported from Latin America, especially Mexico, for decades before the practice was outlawed. New parrot owners eventually realized that parrots, being intensely social and intensely needy of bonds with those around them, make poor pets for anyone other than the most devoted pet owner. They released their pets, or perhaps just didn't mind if they flew away. In some cases, individuals of the same species found each other and started a new population far north of their natural range. Some of the parrot species whose populations are increasing in the Los Angeles basin are threatened with extinction in their native lands. So, in addition to embracing these birds as symbols of subtropical wildness in suburbia, we should also recognize that LA may have inadvertently provided a refuge and reservoir for several beautiful species that are disappearing from their ancestral homes.

We know a great deal about the parrots of the Los Angeles basin, in part because of efforts by ornithologist Kimball Garrett, of the Natural History Museum of Los Angeles County, and his colleagues. For the past twenty-five years Garrett's team has observed, monitored, and compiled information about all the nonnative parrots in our area. It's a somewhat thankless task, because few in the scientific community are interested in nonnative animals. And as we saw, the public is split between fascination and annoyance, with some occasional anger in the mix.

The most abundant Los Angeles parrot is the red-crowned parrot (*Amazona viridigenalis*), sometimes referred to as the green-cheeked parrot. This foot-long species is bright green with even brighter green checks, a scarlet pate, and a violet nape. It flashes red in the wings and yellow in the tail when in flight. The red-crowned parrot is a truly beautiful bird, and today its population in the United States, mostly in the San Gabriel Valley, is north of several thousand parrots, possibly outnumbering the remaining red-crowned populations in northeastern Mexican forests. This species was reported in southern Texas long before it established itself in Southern California, probably wandering north across the border in search of food during drought years. Red-crowned parrots are known in their native lands to nest in woodpecker holes in tree trunks, and they did the same on occasion in Texas. Like most parrots, the red-crowned loves fruit, and will fly many miles a day in search of ripe fruit trees.

Large flocks can ravage crops of avocados, dates, pecans, almonds, and other fruit crops.

The second-most-seen large parrot, at least in the Pasadena area, is the lilac-crowned parrot (*A. finschi*), a lovely bird very similar in size and color to the red-crowned. It hails from hilly country in western Mexico, flocking in groups of two to three hundred, although those numbers are in decline. Unsurprisingly, its crown is lilac in color, backing a patch of bright red just behind its huge beak. It has a somewhat more subdued personality than the red-crowned, though this could be an effect of smaller numbers. Like their red-crowned relatives, lilac-crowned parrots are known in Mexico as crop raiders.

The closely related red-lored parrot (*A. autumnalis*) is similar in appearance to both the other species and also occurs in small numbers in our area. Its native range is from northeastern Mexico to northernmost South America; it was formerly very abundant in the state of Veracruz and is still seen flying around the famed Mayan ruins of Tikal in Guatemala.

These three species, along with very small numbers of a few other Amazons, are the parrots we see crossing the sky in small flocks all day, and leaving or arriving at nighttime roosts in huge numbers. Yellow-headed Amazons (*A. oratrix*), an iconic pet parrot species, isn't as common in my area as it once was, although I've recently spotted a few in suburban trees near the mountain front.

In addition to the big parrots, many smaller parrots and parakeets now call the Los Angeles basin their home. The most common is a pretty South American bird called the mitred parakeet (*Aratinga mitrata*), native to central and southern South America, well south of the equator. This species and its relatives are known in the pet trade as conures, and they're seen in large, noisy flocks all over Los Angeles, from the beach towns to downtown to the San Gabriel Valley, and even Orange County. In Pasadena, they often gather in huge fig trees. Unlike the big parrots, most conures are still quite abundant in their native homelands, where they are considered agricultural pests.

Conures have a much slenderer build than Amazon parrots, with long, pointed tails adding to their length. The mitred parakeet is bright green with a crimson mottled face mask around the eyes. The very closely related and similar-looking red-masked parakeet *(A. erythrogenys)* is the only other parakeet that I've seen often in the Pasadena area. It is native to coastal parts of Ecuador and Peru and is much less common, but it is hard to distinguish from the mitred without a close-up look, and the two species sometimes flock together. Several other parakeets call Los Angeles home these days, including the lovely black-hooded "nanday conure" *(Nandayus nenday)* from southern South America, which I've seen in the canyons leading down to the beach in Pacific Palisades and other areas of the west side of LA.

A few other parakeets are worth mentioning. The little yellow-chevroned *(Brotogeris chiriri)* and white-winged *(B. versicolurus)* parakeets from the Amazon basin are so similar that they need careful observation to distinguish them. They're closely related and some experts have argued that they're geographic variants of one and the same species in their expansive native range in Latin America. But in Los Angeles, the two don't seem to hybridize—and the yellow-chevroned far outnumbers the white-winged. The former is often seen clambering in the crowns of silk floss trees *(Ceiba speciose),* ripping apart their huge seed pods. I've seen them in the heart of downtown Los Angeles, anywhere a silk floss is planted. The rose-ringed parakeet *(Psittacula krameri)* has a huge natural distribution across Africa and South Asia, and is a truly lovely bird also valued in the pet trade. A pair nested on my street in South Pasadena some years ago, but they're more common in the coastal cities. I've seen this parakeet many times in India, where it is an iconic species of gardens, temples, and villages. The rose-ringed is the only common Los Angeles parrot not from Latin America.

Other parrots are occasionally seen flying over Los Angeles suburbia or sitting in a backyard tree: cockatiels, budgies, even giant white-crested cockatoos or, rarely, majestic macaws. But these are random, rare escapees—not established populations. My guess is that macaws and cockatoos have so much value in the pet trade that escaped birds are often captured to be sold or kept. Laws protect animals from abuse, and prohibit the capture of all native birds, but there is a bit of a gray zone when it comes to the status of nonnative birds that could be construed as pests.

A question worth asking: why have the species in the above accounts become established in Southern California while others haven't? And second: why are a few species so common (even dominant?) while others exist only in small numbers? Random chance explains why certain species occur here at all: of the many species that are imported and sold for the pet trade, only a few have escaped or been released in large enough numbers to find each other and start breeding. A nonrandom factor may be climate; some equatorial parrots are more delicate about temperature and humidity than others, since in the tropical lowlands their species never experience temperatures approaching freezing. Our locally established species, like the red-crowned, tend to hail from subtropical areas that experience Los Angeles–level climate extremes, and thus are likely better able to tolerate a severe winter chill. Some species may specialize on particular fruit or seed species in their native lands, or may have narrow nesting requirements—like a particular-sized tree or tree cavity, as most parrots nest in holes in tree trunks—which limits them from establishing a self-sustaining population here. And others, like macaws and cockatoos, may be just so darn valuable in dollars that their owners take greater care not to accidentally or intentionally liberate them.

The presence of all these parrots in our neighborhoods is a gift, even if not every resident sees it that way. People's most common critique is that parrots are not native, they don't contribute to the local ecology, and so we shouldn't care about their fate. Yet, the entire ecosystem in which they live is nonnative. Furthermore, parrots disperse seeds of many trees far and wide, even if these are mostly nonnative trees. I have never once, in many years hiking our local canyons, spotted a flock of exotic parrots feasting in a native tree. In fact, I've never even seen them flying through our local canyons. Their "natural" habitat in Los Angeles is the suburban groves of exotic fig trees, carobs, date palms, and the rest that are so densely planted that the parrots never lack for food. In an unnatural landscape, some of the alterations we've made are relatively harmless and certainly beautiful. Parrots, a raucous intelligence aloft on colorful wings, bring more color and delight into our lives, and we're the better for it.

II.

DANGEROUS, OR MISUNDERSTOOD?

7

Wily and Wildly Successful

Most nights, coyotes prowl and howl in my neighborhood. When they vocalize, it's usually not just a random, lonely howl; more often, it sounds like three to five coyotes yipping together. Occasionally, there are audible brawls—two packs fighting over something, or perhaps a pack mixing it up with a local dog. I live two hundred yards from the edge of a canyon, and the coyotes may well be crossing the canyon from the San Gabriel Mountains to forage for supper in my neighborhood. This typical LA scene is played out across North America. Coyotes have a presence in New York City, including Manhattan, where they eke out an existence hunting for house cats and other small mammals and foraging in garbage cans for human leftovers. A stable population of a dozen or so is reported to inhabit Golden Gate Park in San Francisco.

The coyote is a widespread, ubiquitous North American carnivore, quintessentially independent and wild, but also utterly dependent on humans. Depending on whom you talk to, it's a clever, beautiful canine that we should appreciate, even celebrate, as a bit of wildness in our suburbs. Or, it's a dangerous, disease-carrying scourge of our neighborhoods, posing a threat to unsuspecting pets and even children. In fact, both views have validity, though I would come down firmly on the "embrace them as local wildlife" side.

For many Americans, from ranchers to city dwellers, coyotes are to twenty-first-century life what wolves were to the nineteenth century: undesirable and potentially dangerous vermin. While wolves have ascended a pedestal to celebrity status among most Americans, coyotes have slunk down close to last place in popularity among suburbanites.

Coyotes didn't always live in such close proximity to people. Lewis and Clark reported "prairie wolves" in the western plains and mountains throughout their expedition, though they didn't know the Aztec-derived name for the canid in Mexico, which later spread north. The love-hate (mostly hate) relationship most Americans have with coyotes goes back to the earliest European settlers on the prairie, when barbed wire fences were lined with coyote trophies after one ate a few of a rancher's chickens or lambs. Until well into the twentieth century, coyotes remained iconic animals of the American West. At that point, after a long evolutionary history as a prairie wolf, the species crossed the Mississippi and began colonizing the eastern United States and southern Canada, and a century later had established itself in every one of the continental United States and all the Canadian provinces. This is one adaptable dog.

I've seen coyotes all over the Western United States, and also in rural Mexico. They look like two different animals; the Mexican coyotes, loping past ocotillo and creosote bush, are small, scrawny, and tan, with short-haired coats. Our California suburban coyotes usually appear well nourished, sporting a coat that would rival a German shepherd's. The first time I saw coyotes in Los Angeles, crossing the front lawn of a friend's home as I stepped outside for a morning walk, I took them for largish dogs. They stood slightly shorter at the shoulder than a shepherd, with lovely thick fur of subtle color bands and blends of brown, tan, black, and white. Coyotes are striking animals whose beauty is context dependent—like pigeons, whose purple iridescence is gorgeous but not what stands out when they're pecking around in the gutter. Coyotes' golden meadow–colored fur looks glamorous on a mountain ridge near Pasadena but not as much when rummaging through garbage cans in downtown LA.

As Dan Flores points out in his wonderful book *Coyote America*, the cultural narrative about the coyote has shifted: from the chicken-and-livestock-stealing varmints of the plains—many millions were shot and poisoned by ranchers to no avail—to the marauders of suburban and urban America, invading the gene pools of both wolves and domestic dogs.

In the old days, wolves worried our ancestors at night as a threat to livestock and children. But in the wilds of Yellowstone National Park, extermination of wolves in the last century led to a boom in the coyote population. The wolves were reintroduced into that magnificent ecosystem in the 1990s, and have since cut coyote numbers back down to size. Wolves attack and kill unwary coyotes that try to steal scraps from elk carcasses while the wolves are still feeding. They even enter coyote dens to drag out pups and kill them. But the smaller canids continue to thrive in a vast ecosystem with minimal human contact, presumably coexisting with their dangerous larger kin much as they had for millions of years before the wolf population was slaughtered.

It's very likely that this competitive dynamic between wolves and coyotes also once characterized Southern California. Coyotes, or at least a very similar ancestral form of them, are common in the bones of the La Brea Tar Pits. They coexisted thousands of years ago with dire wolves, the much larger ancient relatives of modern timber wolves. Wolves disappeared from our region by the start of the twentieth century, after which coyotes enjoyed a life free from risk of being killed by their powerful cousins.

Today, the urban/suburban coyote is a massive success story. Coyotes that make a living foraging in suburban neighborhoods live longer and occur in higher densities than those in more natural habitats. While stories of leaping ten-foot fences are likely apocryphal, coyotes can certainly scale the average six-footers that Angelenos erect to demarcate their properties. Wolf urine is marketed online as a coyote preventative, but many a coyote has pranced over urine-soaked lawns to snatch house cats. There are people who dread coyotes, and there are people who provide them with water in the dry summertime. Human LA residents have shot, poisoned, and stoned coyotes. They also offer them dog food (feeding local coyotes is possibly the worst thing one can do), widely photograph them, and brag about them to friends in other cities who don't have wild dogs roaming through their neighborhoods.

A recent study by Rachel Larson and colleagues of coyote habits in the Los Angeles area compared the lives of coyotes in urban, suburban, and more rural neighborhoods. They analyzed their diets, both through their droppings and also through biochemical traces of food in the whiskers of coyotes that had been live-trapped or discovered dead. The researchers found that human food composed a large part of the urban coyote diet. Apparently, dumpster diving works well for them. They also subsisted on tabby cats, sometimes grabbed from under their owners' noses, and the fruits and seeds of figs and other varieties of nonnative trees and plants. Squirrels, gophers, and rabbits, which are significant in the diets of rural and suburban coyotes, didn't figure much at all in the urban coyote diet. In the suburbs, diets shifted seasonally; suburban coyotes ate more human foods in the dry summer months and had a more diverse diet than those who were rural or urban, likely because they had the best of both worlds at their disposal.

In many places where humans regard coyotes as the most dangerous animals, there have been no attacks on humans in recorded history, despite a many-fold increase in coyote populations. Only one fatal attack has ever been recorded in the entire United States, and it occurred in the Los Angeles suburb of Glendale some forty years ago, when a coyote attacked and killed a three-year-old girl. According to one study, there were 142 reported attacks on people in the United States and Canada between 1960 and 2016. Most of these took place in the western US, with half in California. Attacks were as likely to target adults as children, although one-third of all attacks considered to be predatory targeted children—presumably in which the coyote was deemed to be actually hunting prey. A more local estimate exists of 69 coyote attacks in Los Angeles County between 2012 and 2022.

In a recent series of attacks, one or more coyotes living in Elysian Park near Dodger Stadium and downtown LA bit twelve people in 2015 alone, mostly unprovoked. The fact that all the bites happened within a short time window in a small area suggests the attacker was a lone aggressive coyote that had lost its fear of people. Like most coyote attacks, these happened either near the victim's home or in a park.

The number of coyote attacks across North America in more than a half century is dwarfed by the number of shark attacks in United States waters over the same period (about 1,500), and by attacks by both grizzly and black bears (more than 500 during the period). Your chances of being injured or killed by a lightning strike are on the whole far greater than being attacked by a coyote, even in areas where coyote attacks are most common.

Just as the usual scenario for a bear attack begins with human food being accessible to bears, the minor risk of coyote attack can be mitigated, if not eliminated, by avoiding feeding coyotes. Don't, for example, leave dog or cat food outdoors. During recent wildfires here in Southern California, many people put out water bowls intended to support wildlife displaced from their habitats. Of course, the water also attracted coyotes, and—however well-intentioned—increased the chances of negative encounters that could lead to more pressure to trap or eradicate coyotes. Experimental practices of coyote deterrence like "hazing," in which bright lights, shouting, and arm-waving are said to keep them away from homes, are often advocated without any evidence of success. Peaceful coexistence between humans and coyotes happens by leaving the animals to their own devices.

Over the past few decades, the human population of the Los Angeles basin has increased dramatically, and the suburbs have pushed their way farther and farther into the mountains and canyons in which coyotes have roamed for millennia. As it has been with LA's other large carnivores, we've taken ourselves to them as much as they've come to us. Meanwhile, while we have no real estimate of the local coyote population, it appears to be increasing; the statewide population is estimated at more than a half million. When people trap coyotes to remove them from an area, studies have found that other coyotes replace them quickly, and females produce larger litters when the local coyote population wanes. Coyotes will likely be more abundant in the future, forcing us to think about new ways to coexist peacefully with an impressively adaptable large carnivore.

As I wrote these last paragraphs, while glancing out my living room windows, a coyote appeared, walking calmly down the sidewalk a few yards away. I went to the front porch to get a better look and snap a photo. The coyote had his tail between his legs, his ears laid low. Then I saw why. He was a very sick animal, his once lustrous multitoned coat mostly gone, a raw red patch of skin on his rump. He gave me a look, surveyed his surroundings, and continued a slow walk down the street toward parts unknown. A sick or injured coyote is not a rare sight, telling us that life for this smart, adaptable carnivore is tough in a human setting.

8

Beloved,
Cuddly Killers

As a young cat, Toby loved to lounge around my well-planted yard, playing hide-and-seek with himself in tall native grasses and shrubs. There was a birdbath in a little fern garden outside my home office window, so I could distract myself with the comings and goings of everything from warblers to hawks. I had paved the area under the birdbath with rough stones, deterring Toby from lying in wait for birds that innocently came to drink. It had always worked. Then, one winter there was an influx of pine siskins—small finches that spend most of their lives in the mountains but occasionally migrate downslope during winter in massive numbers to suburban backyards. That winter was an irruptive year for siskins, and I had thirty or forty at my feeders every day. Toby realized quickly—before I did—that siskins are unwary little birds and not wary at all while at the birdbath. I discovered this all too vividly when I went into the backyard one day and found Toby playing with not one but several siskin trophies. Mea culpa. That was the end of his predatory days, and of my days allowing a house cat to venture outdoors.

Domestic cats are among the most environmentally destructive animals in our Southern California landscape. A 2012 study estimated that our beloved tabbies kill between one and four billion birds in North America each year. *Billions*, not millions. We don't have statistics for the Los Angeles area, but given the human population and the popularity of cat ownership in suburbia, we can be sure that it's an appalling total. In addition to birds, house cats kill between six and twenty-two billion mammals annually. Add in hundreds of millions of native reptiles and amphibians. That's not merely predation: it's a slaughter of our native wildlife at the hands of nonnative animals. Cat lovers, and animal advocates in general, don't like to acknowledge the scale of the mortality; they argue that other causes of death to songbirds, like flying into buildings or poisoning by pesticides, are more consequential. But the actual evidence shows that house cats who hunt outdoors may be driving the extinction of many species. It's not just common backyard birds, either. Tired and hungry migrating birds that land in suburban yards, seeking a respite before resuming their flight of thousands of kilometers between breeding and wintering grounds, become lunch for local cats.

Domestic cats in suburban Los Angeles fall into three categories: indoor pet cats, pet cats that are allowed outdoors but consider one house, or even two, to be their home, and cats that belong to no one and live their lives entirely outdoors as wild animals, fearful of people. These feral cats, according to studies, are the worst of the worst when it comes to predation on our native wildlife. Lacking a human-provided food supply, they are highly efficient hunters in and around areas of human habitation.

The Los Angeles feral cat population is very difficult to census—is a cat feral if it occasionally shows up on various porches to eat food that someone put out for it? The number has been estimated at between sixty and one hundred million cats across North America. In Los Angeles, a city of four million people, there are perhaps three million cats, a substantial percentage of which hunt outdoors either full-time or part-time.

A pernicious cycle appears to keep the feral population in Los Angeles and elsewhere so large. Cat owners abandon unwanted litters of kittens without spaying or neutering. Males grow into fearsome feral cats that control territories and spend their lives hunting for birds, small mammals, and unspayed female cats. The resulting kittens are basically wild animals, and the feral cat population grows. It may even be the case that unneutered male cats are more likely than females to be dumped by pet owners, because they spray to mark their territory and are eager to roam. The genetic basis for wildness in domestic cats, so much an attractive part of their personas for many owners, works against them, since those males that spray and are skittish are likelier to end up feral, passing their wily genes on to a new generation of feral kittens.

Because feral cats are skilled hunters like other wild cats, they can devastate an ecosystem full of animals that did not evolve in concert with intense predator pressure. Islands in particular are vulnerable. Feral tabby cats on the Channel Islands off the coast of Southern California devastated seabird populations by devouring chicks for decades. Removal of the cats by poisoning or shooting was hotly opposed by animal welfare groups. While the battle between environmental biologists and animal rights advocates raged, the invasive cats killed thousands more endangered birds and small mammals. Finally, a compromise solution was reached: expert trappers using humane methods removed more than sixty cats and kittens from the islands and rehomed them in an animal sanctuary on the mainland. This process cost millions more than inhumane removal (poisoning or shooting) but was well worth the increased public support for the project. In the absence of cats, populations of native Channel Islands small mammals are recovering, and migrating songbirds are far safer.

Other countries have gone to draconian lengths to try to eliminate the environmental scourge of feral cats. In Australia, feral tabbies have caused the extinction of some twenty species of small mammals and birds, and they threaten the survival of hundreds more. Australia has responded by declaring war on feral cats through trapping (humanely or otherwise), by airdropping poisoned baits, and even by shooting. In New Zealand, home to several iconic flightless birds like the kiwi, wildlife advocates have called for a ban on cat ownership.

Cats start breeding as early as six months of age and can each produce several litters of several kittens per year—close to rabbit-level reproductive output. Some rescue centers in Southern California and throughout the US humanely trap and rehabilitate feral cats to become adoptable. But these efforts cannot begin to cope with the enormous numbers of feral cats across North America devastating native wildlife. Another popular approach has been trap, neuter, and return, or TNR. TNR operates on the premise that if you remove a feral cat from its territory, another feral cat will simply move in and replace it. So instead, the feral cat is cage-trapped, brought to a clinic and neutered, then released at the same spot in which it was captured. Some of the cats are adopted out rather than released, and TNR has reduced the number of feral cats in shelters, and therefore lessened the need to euthanize large numbers of ferals each year. In theory, the number of feral cats ought to decline over time.

Unfortunately, there is no evidence that the feral population actually does decline; the number of cats trapped and neutered is too small to make a major impact. Moreover, there is little evidence that a feral cat is actually able to exclude more ferals from taking up residence in its territory. Instead, TNR potentially maintains feral cat populations in perpetuity. It is a plan rooted in a concern for animal welfare, not environmental biology. In environmental terms, the feel-good outcome of not euthanizing unwanted cats has no benefit for the billions of wild songbirds devoured by cats each year.

There is deep hypocrisy in the way we Angelenos deal with our stray cat population. Animal rights organizations that advocate every pet's right to life and both physical and psychological well-being also advocate spaying and neutering. I support spaying and neutering as much as anyone, but we rarely admit to ourselves that our lovable household castrated male or spayed female tabby has been deprived of one of its most basic life impulses and purposes. The image of thousands of euthanized cats is a terrible one. The image of a literal mountain of carcasses of the native songbirds and other small animals they kill each year ought to be even more terrible, but for most people it is not. Educating cat owners may mitigate the harm that feral cats cause. Angelenos would likely not tolerate the extreme cat eradication measures taken in other countries. But there's hypocrisy in cat owners saying they are motivated by a compassion for animals while allowing their pets outdoors to kill again and again. Apparently, compassion does not extend to the billions of our native animals lost each year to domestic cats.

We all know that our little tabby cats are efficient, ruthless predators on smaller animals. It is as deep in their DNA as language is in ours. We see it when they curl their bodies into a sinewy ball, then launch themselves at a cat toy. We find it gruesomely impressive and curious when they bring a treasure they've caught, a mouse or grasshopper, into the house and drop it at our feet. We like to think that in their little cat minds they've thoughtfully brought their owner a gift, when in all likelihood they just consider their house a safe refuge in which to store their kill before consuming it at their leisure.

We love our cats for their graceful lines and sinuosity, for their propensity to belie that grace with profoundly odd behavior at times, and for their affection that is so much harder to earn than that of a tongue-lolling, tail-wagging puppy. Their enormous dilatory pupils seem to display wisdom, love, fear, anger, curiosity—though it's likely that only some of these tendencies even exist in a cat's mind. We anthropomorphize our dogs, but we aggrandize our cats. When you think about it, cats are one of the stranger animals on the planet to become domesticated thousands of years ago. The intense symbiosis between dogs and people is easy to understand. Wolves and dogs are highly social animals, needy for companionship, a pack to call their own. But a solitary, highly independent animal like a wild cat evolving in the hands of humans into a cuddly lap pet is an unlikely journey. Devote ten thousand years to selectively breeding raccoons, opossums, or minks for cuddliness and docility and you'd likely have a far better candidate for a beloved household pet than a tabby cat. But cats are what we have, and we have a responsibility to consider more than our adoration of them when facing the reality of our pets' impacts on the living creatures with whom we share our world.

9

Little Chewers

The city of Los Angeles was recently named, for the second year in a row, the second rattiest city in the United States. We can't scream "We're Number One" because Chicago still takes top honors, with New York City in third place. It makes a lot of sense that Los Angeles and environs are rat infested. Our climate stays warm enough in winter for the little rodents to keep breeding and foraging unabated.

Of all the animals Angelenos share their lives with, rats and mice are no doubt the most ever present. No matter how much time, effort, and money you spend rat-proofing your home, they will find a way in. Rodent exterminators run a brisk business year-round. In my 1912-built redwood home, hearing creepy evidence of rats inside the walls was not uncommon; their wood-gnawing was audible. We could seal up the crawl spaces and roof all we liked, but summer evenings on the back deck still sometimes starred the silhouette of a rat sprinting across the power lines from the trees to our roof. We joked they were "dwarf possums" to guests from colder climes, who found it repulsive to see a rodent while eating dinner.

As a species, we humans are dwarfed by the size of the global rodent population, which is certainly in the tens of billions. The rats and mice that share our lives are the modern tips of great rodent radiations that spread across the globe during prehistoric times. In the Eocene period some fifty million years ago, we see the first fossil evidence of puny mammals that would someday be classified as rodents. Their adaptability was the script for an evolutionary success story that may have expedited the extinction of their predecessors, the small, skulking Plesiadapid mammals that previously occupied the niche of small, furry mammal. The Plesiadapids looked a bit like squirrels but had some evolutionary affinities to the earliest primates. They thrived around the time of the extinction of the dinosaurs, then went extinct around the time of the rise of the rodents.

However it happened, the rodents are a phenomenal success, from the hulking capybara, the world's largest rodent, weighing up to seventy-five kilograms and a denizen of Amazon rivers and streams, to the African pygmy mouse, measuring two inches long and weighing just a few grams. Their global spread and diversity of sizes and shapes rivals those of any mammalian order. Rodents occur naturally on every continent except Antarctica, and in many places reach astronomical densities.

In the Los Angeles basin, we are "graced" with two rat species. The brown or Norway rat *(Rattus norvegicus)* is the common rat in most of Southern California, and indeed the whole world. It's the stereotypical street rat, the species dragging the pizza slice through a New York City subway station or scampering along a gutter in Beijing or Paris. Once, walking at night along a broken sidewalk in Indonesia, I was besieged by feral cats begging for food handouts. I reached down in the dark to pet one of them, and a complacent-looking brown rat tilted his head and stared up at me. Rats in urban areas are, you could say, accustomed to people.

The brown rat is a robust species, the largest reaching a half kilo in weight and nearly a foot in length, with a long, scaly tail that can add almost another foot. This is the species that scientists have bred a million times over for laboratory experiments. Ironically, there have been stunningly few studies of rats' natural behavior outside the lab to help us better understand their in-lab behavior. Ancestors of this species also gave rise to the pet rats sold the world over. Brown rats tend to be terrestrial, preferring the local storm sewer or garage crawl space to roofs and trees.

The other ubiquitous Los Angeles rat is the roof rat (Rattus rattus). Smaller and more gracile than the brown rat, the roof rat is the rodent that, at least in the Pasadena area where I lived, moves into walls, attics, and ceiling crawl spaces. These rats are also the ones you see crossing power lines between trees, or making nests high above the ground in the old thatch of palm trees. To say they're ubiquitous is an understatement. My urban university campus office had a rat problem for years following a remodel that left interior spaces accessible. The exterminators first identified the paths of the rodents' perambulations in the crawl space above the ceiling tiles of my office, then placed many baits traps along that path. The daily sound of rat claws scratching and scampering above decreased, but didn't stop. The situation came to a head when one day, as I sat in my office having a conference with a student, a ceiling tile above our heads tilted and a large rat dropped onto the carpet right between us, then wobbled slowly into the corner of my office, likely poisoned.

While rats are the most obvious rodents infesting the lives of Angelenos, they are likely outnumbered in sheer quantity by mice. The house mouse (Mus musculus) lives nearly the world over. European colonizers unintentionally introduced it to North America starting in the early sixteenth century. The same species has since been bred in the billions for laboratory research, for the pet trade, and for pet food. Their interest to science is such that the house mouse genome was mapped early on, some twenty years ago. As medical models go, mice are useful; the DNA sequence of a house mouse is more than 80 percent the same as that of humans. Mice in general are more closely related to us than a host of other mammals. After tree shrews, rabbits, colugos (flying lemurs), and nonhuman primates, rodents are our closest kin. And we seem to feel some affinity for them, judging by how often they've been characters in our fantasies (Mickey and Minnie of Disney lore, and the Mouse King in the Nutcracker—a nightmarishly big house mouse—to name a few).

House mice may be miniature versions of the more destructive rats, but they are well capable of inflicting property damage out of scale to their size, as well as spreading diseases, usually via parasitic lice and fleas that hitchhike on their bodies. An outbreak of hantavirus in Yosemite National Park in 2012—spread by vapors and dust from dried excrement of deer mice—infected nine visitors staying in the historic tent cabins in the valley, plus another victim presumed infected while camping or hiking. Three of the ten infected visitors died, and the entire camp of nearly a hundred cabins was demolished. This was the second hantavirus outbreak in the western United States since 1990; the first, in the Four Corners region, killed twenty-seven of forty-eight infected people. A few cases are reported annually, with about a 35 percent mortality rate. Hantavirus is, like the coronavirus with which we have all become all too familiar, a zoonotic disease that leaps from rodents into human hosts. And as with some other notorious diseases in human history, small rodents are the vectors.

The California deer mouse *(Peromyscus californicus)* was the culprit behind the Yosemite and other hantavirus outbreaks, a Southern California and Northern Mexico native. The species is famous among biologists for being one of the very few truly monogamous mammals on Earth. A male and female will form a lifelong bond, ignoring other potential mates and coparenting to rear their offspring. Although deer mice typically don't invade your house and live in your walls (more commonly they reside in woodpiles and sheds), they will quickly find a bin of birdseed left uncovered in your garage. Given their hantavirus connection, there's a strong incentive to keep them out of human habitations.

While the house mouse and deer mouse are the most common mice in the Los Angeles basin, white-footed mice *(Peromyscus leucopus)* inhabit wooded areas like Griffith Park and local canyons, along with other mouse-like rodents. The California vole *(Microtus californicus)* is a stubby-tailed little rodent often mislabeled "meadow mouse." Many California homeowners with lawns or fields have experienced the hole havoc wreaked by gophers. Botta's pocket gopher *(Thomomys bottae)* is our local gopher, and its appetite for underground roots and shoots is truly infamous. The network of tunnels gophers hollow out just beneath an expensively groomed lawn can cover a thousand square feet and extend several feet underground. Unfortunately for lawn owners, tunnels tend to have surface openings all around the yard. This fuels efforts to eradicate gophers; many resort to poisoning or even spearing them. Considering that gophers are the long-term residents of the turf and the homeowners the interlopers, there's a tragic irony to that approach.

Fact is, gophers are highly territorial, so they space themselves out across a flat area, reaching a maximum density of about thirty gophers per acre. That means that just a few populate the average suburban tract, though even those few can destroy the green, oceanic serenity of a lawn that humans are so perversely proud of. Most gardeners put wire mesh around their plots to keep gophers at bay, or simply resort to raised garden beds.

But consider the upside of gophers. If you're more interested in a natural landscape than a heavily watered, thick green lawn—and if you're reading this book you probably are—gophers contribute to the health of that more natural ecosystem. Their holes aerate soil and prevent compaction, promoting the growth and health of native trees. Their burrows provide shelter for wildlife we'd like to encourage, like lizards and even burrowing owls in more rural areas.

Rodents also play an important role in natural ecosystems as the prey base for larger carnivores. In Los Angeles, where nonnative species have largely displaced native ones, the nonnative mice and rats still occupy that prey role. But the subsidies of human detritus have led to a population explosion that makes mice and rats far too abundant for any population of bobcats, hawks, ravens, coyotes, and even house cats to contain.

So, what do we do about the rodent population? Beyond being more careful about trash containment, kill-trapping and poisoning are typical remedies. Poisoning has long been people's preferred option for killing rats in our most populated areas, but this carries the risk of sickening or killing other animals too. In the Santa Monica Mountains, many bobcats, coyotes, and even a few mountain lions have been unintentionally poisoned. Hawks and owls that prey on small mammals are also likely to poison themselves by eating rats. The effects of rat poison are not limited to nonhuman animals. Thousands of children living near rodent populations are also accidentally sickened, according to one government estimate.

Here in Los Angeles, the sale of rodent-killing poisons has been regulated. The most popular brands, which cause fatal internal bleeding after a single-dose ingestion, are outlawed, although homeowners still order products online that are no longer sold in stores. A less immediately lethal version is just as bad, because it may leave the rat in a sickened but still mobile condition, allowing it to stagger into your yard and become a poisonous meal for your dog or cat. Traps don't carry these risks; some kill by spring action and others zap electronically. But poisons are still in use, and in all likelihood the harmful effects they have on our ecosystem are not fully known. A new rodent contraceptive offers hope—it renders female rats and mice less fertile and also disrupts male rodent sperm production. And it won't harm our pets or local wildlife, according to the manufacturers.

Despite all rodent-preventative measures, rats and mice are more visible in the Los Angeles basin today than ever. The COVID-19 pandemic brought widespread restaurant and food outlet shutdowns, and the ensuing lack of food waste deprived rats of their major food source. This may have fueled the apparent surge in rat sightings in and around homes; as a lack of food caused rodent populations to decline, it also forced them to become more brazen. There were even reports of rats cannibalizing each other. It's a rat-eat-rat world out there, and the rodents' adaptability is simply stronger than our capacity to make serious inroads to curb their huge populations.

10

Don't Let the Green Grass Fool You

The suburban lawn is a manifestation of the human soul's need for a bit of green space in a sea of pavement, steel, and glass. The suburban lawn is also an environmentally terrible and aesthetically ghastly attempt to obtain that sense of bucolic tranquility.

These two statements are equally true. As a hallowed icon of suburbia, the lawn has been the subject of many books. Armchair scholars have argued that there is something comforting to the psyche about a park-like landscape of grass and scattered trees that replicates the tree-dotted savannas in which our earliest ancestors lived. Most agree that the modern lawn is the descendant of the green, grassy expanses of eighteenth-century European aristocrats' estates, maintained by grazing sheep, and later urban parks that functioned as the lungs of teeming East Coast cities. The lawn concept later crept into more ordinary residential settings. Eventually, a smooth, emerald-green postage stamp became a symbol of financial success, and Americans began to take exceptional, sometimes fetishistic, pride in having the tidiest patch of green on the block.

The cultural history of lawns in Southern California is fascinating, revealing residents' willful ignorance of the landscape. But the ecological history of lawns is downright disturbing, especially in light of climate change and an increasingly water-poor environment. You might think that when Los Angeles became suburbanized, the grasses used in lawns were either native varieties or those with drought-tolerant qualities. On the contrary, most of the varieties sold here are thirsty, only looking lush and green under a regimen of regular, copious water. The lion's share of California's water is slated for agriculture. Of the smaller slice that is for residential use, most ends up on lawns and gardens, and in pools and hot tubs. Not surprisingly, water use in the Los Angeles area follows the money. Lower-income neighborhoods may use as little as fifty gallons per household per day, while affluent communities may use ten times that amount. Typically, lawn watering in Southern California accounts for half to two-thirds of total household water consumption.

In addition to the vast quantities of precious water wasted in lawns, vast quantities of toxic fertilizer and pesticides enter our food chain and poison children and pets. Sixty years after Rachel Carson's *Silent Spring*, homeowners who carefully curate their children's diet with kale and quinoa blithely bathe their properties with poisons. Even pesticides that were long considered benign, like Roundup, are now known to be toxic. The megatons of nitrogenous fertilizer applied to lawns also emit nitrous oxide, a greenhouse gas far more potent than carbon dioxide. This means that although lawns are green space that ought in theory to trap carbon from the air and store it, lawns, golf courses, and sports field are actually major sources of greenhouse gases. This doesn't even include the air (and noise) pollution from thousands of gas-powered lawn mowers and leaf blowers operating on any given day across the LA basin.

The lawn is still the default yard in much of North America, but in the arid Southwest, drought-minded homeowners and cities have managed to change the ethos quite a bit. The suburbs of Phoenix and Tucson in particular have embraced alternative lawns; instead of green grass, gravel and cactus decorate neighborhoods. But even that arid region is still dotted with golf courses and their obligatory expanses of thirsty green grass.

If Angelenos are not about to give up their cherished lawns entirely, they can at least plant more water-wise, drought-tolerant varieties of lawn grasses. The grasses marketed to Californians are overwhelmingly nonnative, thirsty plants: Saint Augustine or Bermuda (native to Africa), which tolerates trampling by children's feet, or more delicate-looking, thirstier varieties like Kentucky bluegrass (native to Eurasia). They're basically sterile green rugs.

When I ripped out my lawn and patches of ivy in the 1990s, neighbors politely complained. I was told that my curbside plantings of native California plants were unsightly and that they blocked neighbors' views of the street. Soon after, however, my city began offering rebates per square foot of lawn replaced by drought-tolerant gardens. Drought gardening took hold and lawns began to disappear, until the city's rebate budget ran dry. Today, half the homes on that block either don't have lawns or have partially replaced them. Numerous books and articles have advocated drought-friendly lawn alternatives. The constant threat of megadrought and uncertainty over the future of water in Los Angeles—such as the current battle over taking water from the Colorado River—loom large in this issue. This doesn't mean Southern California is going the xeric (arid) route of Arizona towns, with their cactus and ocotillo gardens. A wide variety of gorgeously showy Southern California plants will thrive in a former lawn converted to an occasionally watered garden, and the result can be a striking upgrade.

If one insists on keeping a lawn, some grass species don't need constant soaking. There is, however, a catch: Most grasses native to Southern California, or to other seasonally dry areas of the southwest, have a long dormant phase each year. Shutting down growth allows them to survive the furnace heat of the long, dry summer, when attempting to put energy into new green flush would only expose them to evaporative water loss. Many a homeowner has planted a native, drought-tolerant garden when the grasses are in green flush in autumn or winter, only to watch it all turn a burnt straw color in summer.

A native Southern California lawn may require some optical adjustments by your neighbors; the burnished appearance of a sweep of local fescues may be an acquired taste. But in addition to being hardy, drought-tolerant, and low-maintenance, many native grasses are beautiful. California fescue *(Festuca californica)* is my favorite example. It's compact and robust, but sends up blades a meter or more high, with flower stalks that flutter in the breeze above them. Blue fescue *(F. glauca)* is everywhere, planted in little crowned clumps along walkways and garden borders. I've never found them very interesting, but they're hardy and tough and extremely popular. Idaho fescue *(F. idahoensis)* and western fescue *(F. occidentalis)* are similar to other fescues but a bit more attractive, although prone like the others to blanch blonde-brown during parched summer months.

This is not to say that native California grasses don't need water. Some of the most desirable species don't do well without regular water, especially while they're growing. A few years ago, I was wowed by a native California grass that had newly appeared my local plant nursery. Point Molate red fescue *(F. rubra)* is a variety of creeping fescue grass native to the San Francisco Bay area, occurring naturally along the bay not far from the Richmond–San Raphael Bridge. As it grows, Point Molate red fescue forms a billowing deep-green sprawl, and when hundreds of them overlap and ripple in a breeze, the effect is beautiful and hypnotic. I planted a few plugs of the grass, watered them well, and they grew nicely. So, I converted a section of my backyard to Point Molate fescue, sat back, and waited for the billowing dune-like waves of fescue grass to take shape. The results were disappointing. Unless it had exactly the right balance of shade, sun, and water, it failed to thrive. After couple of years my new mini-lawn was sparse, only flourishing during winter rains. Point Molate fescue is still sold widely, but the initial excitement over the idea of replicating our lawns with native grasses has been injected with realism.

Some grasses are spectacular landscaping plants in their own right. But some of the most visually striking are also terribly invasive and prone to spreading rapidly, and so should never be planted where they could colonize local hills or canyons. Mexican feather grass *(Nassella tenuissima)* is a hardy, lovely, foot-and-a-half-tall clumping grass whose feathery flower stalks flutter in a light breeze. A sweep of feather grass can be beautiful, but the beauty carries an environmental cost. The seeds are easily spread by wind or birds from the yard to any nearby canyon. Once established, Mexican feather grass crowds out native grasses and is difficult to eradicate.

Fountain grasses *(Pennisetum)* are another beautiful but invasive group seen all over our suburbs. Some are small enough to be dainty, while others grow to truly monstrous proportions. All of them spread like wildfire and can devastate natural ecosystems outside their native range. African fountain grass *(P. setaceum)* is native to North Africa, and has ravaged natural lands in Australia, Hawaiʻi, and increasingly Southern California. A tremendous opportunist, it takes advantage of the natural cycles of forest fires in our local hills and canyons. After a productive forest has burned and before its understory can regrow, fountain grasses move in and blanket the land, turning a forest into an exotic grassland in which the indigenous species no longer can regain a toehold. While not a fountain grass, pampas grass *(Cortaderia selloana)* is a giant from South America that grows rapidly to huge size, with showy, billowing flower stalks, and can also dominate native landscapes.

My personal favorite of the large, showy grasses is the giant wild rye *(Elymus condensatus)*, the largest member of the grass family found in the United States. It grows as a huge cluster of silver spikes sprouting flower stalks, often taller than I am. Growing in a variety of habitats in Southern California, wild rye sends out rhizomes to spread and can easily take over a forest clearing, or one's yard. A cultivar called Prince Canyon wild rye is even more silvery, and has the added benefit of being more compactly built and more easily contained. The other commonly planted large native grass is the group containing deer grass, bull grass, and many other species *(Muhlenbergia spp.)*. The eponymous deer grass, *M. rigens*, is most common, with a finer texture than the giant ryes. In my experience, they need to be pruned carefully and severely or they start to look like a huge out-of-control head of hair.

A grass is a grass due to certain anatomical features. All members of the family Poaceae feature flower stalks with petal-less flowers and sepals. In place of flower petals, grasses have two specialized little leaf-life structures, the palea and the lemma, surrounding and protecting the reproductive parts. Many grains are grasses, as are bamboos. In addition, some members of other plant families make excellent alternative lawns. Native California sedges (genus *Carex*) are not grasses but make, in my experience, excellent four-season lawn replacements. Although we have the image of sedges growing in wet, seepy places, many do quite well with limited watering, especially if they're not in day-long bright sun. They tend to be small, gently spreading into a low-lying crown. The little dune sedge (*C. pansa*) from Northern California is probably the most widely planted of the sedges; I have seen dune sedge lawns that were truly striking.

Beyond the grasses and grass-like plants, a host of other plants can form a lovely green blanket on the space traditionally given to a thirsty grass lawn. Some of these are California natives; most are from regions with Mediterranean climates. Native plants like *Ceanothus*, the so-called California lilac, and manzanitas have varieties that are creeping ground covers rather than towering shrubs.

Lantanas are a favorite of mine. These natives of Latin America are so common as to be banal in Los Angeles, but their hardiness and tendency to bloom nearly year-round endear them to gardeners. Many exotic grasses, like mondo grass (*Ophiopogon spp.*), are marketed as decorative plants for edging a walkway, but serve equally well as the lawn itself. Even succulents like indigenous live-forevers (*Dudleya spp.*) and echeverias work as ground covers, as do herbs like thyme (*Thymus spp.*). There are so many excellent lawn replacements out there that the problem is choosing the right one for your own space and taste.

As I walk through suburban neighborhoods in Los Angeles, every year I see a greater proliferation of artificial turf: that is, plastic fake lawns. As if the scourge of sterile natural lawns weren't bad enough, homeowners are now turning to literal plastic carpets. In some cases, cities are encouraging them as water-use reducers. The tradeoff is a hot plastic wrap that provides nothing but heat to the environment, aside from ease of use for the owner. A plastic lawn to accompany plastic lawn ornaments, plastic hoses, and the sundry plastic objects that fill our daily existence. It's the lawn effect taken to its logical extreme, and a powerful, if unintentional, statement about the possible future. Will the suburbs become a plastic replica of a "natural" landscape, full of fake plants and animals?

I'm an acolyte of the movement to replace our exotic ecosystem and its thirsty plants with one that is more climate appropriate and more drought friendly. I am, however, not a purist: a mix of native plants and some non-natives from similar climates helps conserve water. Mediterranean and Australian plants, including grasses, predominate and thrive under even the harshest Southern California drought conditions. Even a portion of a yard converted to native plants provides not only drought tolerance but also the crucial food base for native insects. Many of us were raised to see green lawns as beautiful. Now, we're learning a very different ethos, and seeing green lawns with sadness, and artificial lawns with disgust. Whatever the historical and cultural roots of the modern lawn, there is no place for them in a world that is heating up and drying out.

11

All That Rattles and Slithers

We were on a lovely family hike in Bear Canyon, an offshoot of the very popular Switzer Canyon in the mountains behind Pasadena. The trail wound up and around a hill with a cliff face on one side, and as we stopped to catch our breath and enjoy the view, my son spotted the baby rattlesnake. It was tightly coiled on a tiny overhang several feet above the ground, inches from my daughter's shoulder. The intense, buzzy rattle that usually warns you of treading too close to was absent; this little guy was too small to have grown a rattle. We all stepped back, then relaxed when we saw how tiny the snake was and how innocuous its intentions. It remained coiled in place, a vivid gray and chocolate bracelet.

Snakes are truly remarkable creatures. Evolved from four-legged ancestors, snakes lost their appendages in favor of a body that can slither into tiny holes and crevices: vital organs squeezed into an ultra-flexible cylinder. And yet among the nearly three thousand species of snake is an incredible diversity of form and function. There are tree climbers and oceanic swimmers and burrowers. They range in size from pencil-thin and less than a foot in length to behemoths of seven meters and one hundred pounds. Some coil tightly around their prey until the soon-to-be-dinner's heart stops, while others simply grab a mouse or frog and start swallowing. Snake diets vary in tandem with their size: from ant eggs and insects to birds and mammals, all the way up to crocodiles and deer.

Encountering a rattlesnake is startlingly common in the canyons of the Los Angeles basin, and sometimes in the neighborhoods near the canyons. Griffith Park, the lungs of Los Angeles squeezed between freeways, has a healthy population of rattlers that also show up in backyards and make their way onto the grounds of the Los Angeles Zoo, where they startle visitors and keepers and on at least one occasion fatally bit a chimpanzee.

Rattlesnakes are wonderfully designed ambush predators. They can sit along a rodent trail for weeks, waiting for the right moment to strike, then follow a trail of scent and body heat as the mortally envenomated mouse staggers off to die somewhere. A rattlesnake delivers its venom quickly, essentially squirting it from the venom glands through slits in the fangs into the bite wound. Venom is a highly specialized proteinaceous digestive fluid, evolved over millions of years to be a rattler's first stage of digestion. The chemical breakdown of the mouse begins before the rodent is even inside the snake's mouth.

There's an oft-quoted myth that it's better to be bitten by a larger rattler than a smaller one because the smaller a venomous snake, the more drop-for-drop potent its venom. In fact, the most dangerous bites are highly associated with two factors: the size (and weight) of the snake that bit you, and your own body weight. A third key factor is where you're bitten: it's better to be bitten on the finger than on the forearm, and small snakes tend to bite small appendages like fingers and toes. People panic, understandably, when bitten by a rattlesnake, and often exaggerate the size of the snake that bit them. Southern Pacific rattlesnakes are medium sized as rattlers go; diamondbacks, especially eastern diamondbacks, are far larger and more dangerous. So, if you're a large-bodied person bitten on the finger by a smallish Southern Pacific rattlesnake, you're going to be in pain and need a hospital visit, but very likely you'll none the worse within a few days. On the other hand, a child bitten by a large adult could be in grave danger unless antivenom is administered promptly.

Rattlesnakes are pit vipers, and most pit vipers deliver a dose of venom with their impressive retractable fangs (unlike some snakes that have much shorter, fixed fangs, and others whose venom is conducted along grooves in their rear teeth). Most (but not all) pit vipers pack a venom that is largely hemotoxic; it quickly attacks and disrupts blood vessels, especially near the site of the bite, and sometimes the entire circulatory system. Massive hemorrhaging and swelling may occur along with intense pain, nausea and vomiting, blurred vision, and labored breathing. Antivenom is mostly composed of antibodies designed to combat the effects of a venomous bite. Some antivenoms treat only one species of snake, while others can be used to treat many.

The fear and revulsion so many people experience at the sight of a snake is so deeply embedded in humans that some scholars consider it innate. Fear of harmless snakes is irrational. Fear of dangerous snakes is not irrational, though it's out of proportion to the actual risk posed by rattlesnakes living among us. Each year about fifty people are bitten by rattlesnakes in Southern California, but this includes bites by captive rattlers being handled carelessly by their owners. The victim count also includes hikers who try to handle a wild rattler and end up with fangs embedded in their hands. There's a gender bias: the vast majority of rattlesnake bites are to men who are pet owners, professional snake handlers, religious celebrants (those rattlesnake cults are real), or just overly macho sorts who like to poke at dangerous things, especially after they've consumed some alcohol. A typical episode that occurred while I was writing this chapter: a man tried to use short barbecue tongs to pick up a backyard rattler at a picnic and ended up in the hospital with a bite wound. When we discount such cases of sheer carelessness, we find that the number of people bitten each year in Southern California is extremely small. Your odds of being killed by a snakebite in the wild are roughly the same as your risk of being killed by fireworks on the Fourth of July, and less than your chances of being killed by lightning or a spider bite.

The majority of rattlesnake bites in Southern California occur in spring and early summer, when snakes are out and about in the warm weather, and hiking trails, golf courses, parks, and backyards are crowded with people. During this time the need for snakebite-savvy medical centers peaks, as does the need for antivenom. Loma Linda University Medical Center, an hour's drive east of downtown Los Angeles or a quick helicopter trip, is the go-to place for treating victims of rattlesnake bites. Researchers at Loma Linda have done a great deal of research on treating the bites of the various rattlesnake species in our area, and if the species that inflicted the bite can be identified, they will have its antivenom on hand.

The Southern Pacific rattlesnake (*Crotalus helleri,* or sometimes *C. oreganus helleri*) is the rattler most commonly seen in the Los Angeles basin. It's a relatively small species, averaging only two to four feet in length, although a four-foot rattler can appear much larger while rattling and striking. It lives from Santa Barbara County south through the Los Angeles area to just south of the Mexican border, and also on some of the Channel Islands offshore. Six other species make their home elsewhere in Southern California, including the larger and near-legendary western diamondback (*C. atrox*) that lends its iconic image to everything from Hollywood westerns to baseball teams. Red diamond rattlesnakes (*C. ruber*) also live in the hills not far from the Los Angeles basin; they are common as near as the Riverside area. Most of the other species in our region are small and secretive and likeliest to be found in desert, brushy, or rocky areas far away from cities. Among them, the famous sidewinder has an odd way of moving, throwing a loop of its coils sideways to propel itself across sand.

There was a time when my now very urban campus of the University of Southern California was a place where one encountered snakes. The collection of the Department of Herpetology at the Natural History Museum of Los Angeles County includes California kingsnakes (*Lampropeltis getula californiae*) and San Diego gopher snakes (*Pituophis catenifer annectens*). Today there isn't natural habitat for them within ten miles. I'm sure that 90 percent of the LA's human population is quite pleased with the loss of snake biodiversity in their neighborhoods. But that other 10 percent fully understand what is now missing. Once you see that all but one species in the Los Angeles basin are harmless, and that all are beneficial to us for their consumption of rats and mice, you develop a more sanguine view of these reptiles.

Gopher snakes are the most common serpents seen while hiking the trails of the Los Angeles basin. They're rarely more than four feet long, but routinely mistaken for much longer; the blur of a brown-and-black stripy rope whizzing away gives an impression of great length. I've had friends swear to me that the brown-and-black snake they saw on a trail was at least ten feet long. Gopher snakes of various types live nearly throughout California and occupy almost every possible habitat, with our local variety occurring from northern Santa Barbara County south to Baja California, and on some of the offshore islands. They tend to be active in the daytime and so are more obvious residents. While they're adapted to spending time underground, including in rodent burrows, they also climb well and raid the nests of birds and squirrels. They eat mainly rodents, including the eponymous gopher, but they'll also take young ground squirrels, small rabbits, and any bird they can catch. When caught by hand, some settle easily and allow a calm inspection of their alert beauty, while others struggle to get free and excrete a smelly poop on their captor. Rarely do they attempt to bite.

Just twenty-some miles from the coastline between Los Angeles and Ventura, the islands of Santa Cruz, Santa Rosa, and, farther out to sea, San Miguel are home to a species of gopher snake that evolved in isolation into a small island form. The Santa Cruz gopher snake (*P. catenifer pumilus*) is an island dwarf, reaching no more than three feet but otherwise resembling the San Diego gopher snake that we see all around the LA basin. This is not a case of an animal's body size simply stunted by a limited food supply. Instead, over millennia of isolation, the snakes evolved into a smaller size, probably in a long-term genetic response to the more limited food resources available on the island.

Garter snakes are the ubiquitous snakes across all of North America, small with a stripe or more lengthwise down their back. Often, a child's first experience of a wild snake is a garter found in the back-yard or near a local pond; they capture and marvel at the innocu-ous little reptile while it writhes and emits a foul-smelling musk in protest. Garter snakes are truly abundant in some areas, but in the Los Angeles basin and surrounding mountains, where two species occur, they are uncommon and may be in decline. The south coast garter snake (*Thamnophis sirtalis infernalis*) is distinct from the many other varieties of garter snake in California, although it continues to share a name with its northern kin, pending further studies of its genetics and evolution. The species is believed to have been much more common and widespread in Southern California in the past. Garter snakes are creatures that generally live near water, feeding on small fish and frogs and other small animals, but suburbanization and urbanization have taken a toll. These days you would be hard pressed to find them regularly anywhere in the LA basin.

The other garter snake in our area, less common regionally but perhaps more common when searched for in the right spots, is the two-striped garter snake (*T. hammondi*), a little brown snake with lengthwise pale stripes on its sides. These snakes are highly aquatic; I've encountered them many times hiking in the San Gabriel Moun-tains, always in or very near a stream. Find a quiet spot beside a mountain stream edged by dense brush and receiving some dappled sunlight; this little snake will surely be hunting close by for fish and frogs. At the first sign of danger, it will dive and swim to safety. I've occasionally seen them on the banks of larger streams, basking or hunting in the open.

Just as the south coast garter snake has disappeared from most of our area with increased suburbanization, the two-striped gar-ter has been extirpated from its former haunts by the loss of undis-turbed, unpolluted streams and ponds. It was likely never common in the basin itself, preferring the surrounding canyons and the water that flows through them. We are poorer for not having them at our doorsteps.

The hands-down most beautiful of Southern California's serpent fauna are the kingsnakes. The most familiar, the California kingsnake (*Lampropeltis getula californiae*, or to some just *L. californiae*), is the species that once could be found right in the center of what is now downtown Los Angeles. The species is still fairly common, though declining, and with luck can be seen in our local habitats. Its beauty lies both in simplicity—usually a bold white-and-black banded snake with a white face—and also in variability. Along the coastal area in Orange County and farther south, a striped morph features solid or broken white lines down the spine, against a surface of jet black. And this is merely one of the California Kingsnake's many patterns. Outside the Los Angeles area, local variants are blotched, striped, dotted, nearly solid black, and display background colors from snow white to banana yellow. Add in the species' utterly docile demeanor and you have a reptile that is not only beloved by many Nature enthusiasts but far too often collected as a pet.

Another kingsnake in our area is the true stunner. Found only in the mountains surrounding our basin, the coast mountain kingsnake (*L. multifasciata*) is a gaudy rainbow of wide scarlet bands alternating with black and white rings, terminating in a black head. Formerly considered just a local variant of the widespread California mountain kingsnake, the coast mountain kingsnake is part of a large complex of kingsnakes that may have evolved their color patterns as mimicry-based protection against protectors. If you look enough like the highly venomous coral snake, predators might just leave you alone. This kingsnake's beauty has been much to its detriment, as collectors, scrupulous and not so scrupulous, have scoured our local mountains for them for years. Coast mountain kingsnakes are secretive, and usually underground or deep in rock crevices, but collectors cruise mountain roads after sunset on moist evenings in spring, when the snakes are out and about. The species is now rare, found mainly in places far from roadways. Wildlife officials and herpetologists keep their locations as well-guarded secrets.

Other, less heralded snakes live in our area too. The lovely California striped racer *(Masticophis l. lateralis)*, also known as the chapparal whipsnake, is a rope-thin, flighty snake that is active mainly in daytime and often seen while hiking or picnicking. They're usually three to four feet long but look longer as they glide through grass and brush. Compared to other snakes, California striped racers are highly alert and convey an air of intelligence, simply because they're active diurnal hunters of lizards, whereas kingsnakes and gophers are more sedentary, nocturnal predators.

A few small snakes in our area are so secretive and inconspicuous that even people living next to a canyon or mountains might not be aware of their existence. The western ringneck snake *(Diadophis punctatus)* is a lovely, thread-thin snake, slate gray with a brilliant orange necklace and underside, that resides near streams and is sometimes seen alongside trails or under rocks and logs. Its cuisine of choice is little invertebrates, worms, small salamanders, and frogs. The tiny California black-headed snake *(Tantilla planiceps)* is small enough to be mistaken for a worm, dwelling underground and dining on insects and invertebrates. According to the little information that we have, it is rare or possibly extirpated in the Los Angeles basin.

Snakes are long gone from our urban and suburban landscapes, except neighborhoods that border wilder, wooded areas. When Los Angeles's native habitats are destroyed or degraded, snakes are often at the very bottom of the list of creatures the public worries about.

But their usefulness to us as rodent eaters, their fascinating biology, and their overall harmlessness ought to outweigh the irrational fears.

On trails in our hills and canyons, people and snakes—including rattlesnakes—will continue to encounter each other regularly in warm weather. As long as people learn a few simple rules of conduct, snakes pose practically no threat to anyone; I for one think meeting a snake is as thrilling as spotting a mountain lion or bear. Next time you see one on a trail in our local hills, behold its beauty and its role in Nature, and consider yourself fortunate that in the middle of a metropolis we can still live among such amazing wildness.

12

Arachnophilia

Spiders. Even I, a confirmed lover of all things that creep and crawl, am not fond of spiders. Once, when I occupied a tiny hut in a Peruvian rainforest, I used a machete to kill a large tarantula that lived in the rafters over my bed. The local people scolded me; tarantulas in your home kill cockroaches and are welcome guests. I received a karmic lesson when dozens of baby tarantulas, miniatures of the adult, scattered from their slain mother's back all across my floor. Certainly, there are arachnophiles among us, even those who love scorpions and large centipedes, but they're an even smaller minority than ophidiophiles—snake enthusiasts. And yet spiders are among the most amazing creatures on our planet in their diversity and adaptations. At a more micro scale than most of us pay attention to, they are fearsome predators in every backyard ecosystem. And, for better or worse, the Los Angeles basin has a surfeit of spider species, both native and introduced.

Understanding something often helps one to overcome revulsion or fear of it, and with that in mind, I've read quite a bit about spiders over the years. They're a large—more than forty thousand species worldwide—and diverse group of creatures that all possess eight legs and anywhere from two to eight eyes. They fashion silk as strong as Kevlar to build homes for themselves, nests for eggs and offspring, and traps for prey, rivaling the engineering abilities of any animal on Earth. Synthesizing venom has helped them occupy the role of fearsome predator on smaller creatures in their habitat.

Like many animals that are mistaken for close relatives because they look alike—seals and sea lions, for example, are not closely related—spiders comprise two groups with widely divergent evolutionary histories. Tarantulas and trapdoor spiders compose one group; orb-weaving, jumping, and wolf spiders are the other. Connections and antecedents among these lineages are still much debated, even with the help of molecular studies of spider genomics. For example, multiple lineages of web-weaving spiders tell us either that orb weaving evolved independently more than once; that all web-making spiders have a common, very ancient ancestor; or that some descendent lineages lost their web-weaving tendencies and then reevolved them.

We are blessed, if you will, with more than two hundred species of spiders in the Los Angeles basin, from the big and hairy tarantula to the dark and sinister widows, to species so tiny and inconspicuous that hardly anyone knows they exist. Most of these spiders are native to California, with a scattering of species introduced unwittingly from Europe or Asia.

 The notorious black and brown widows of the family Theridiidae—the cobweb weavers—are the only dangerous spiders found in Los Angeles suburbia (the infamous brown recluse, while often mistakenly identified in homes, does not occur here). Both species are quite common, their webs occupying our woodpiles, basements, and crawlspaces. They use the sticky webs to catch prey, then envenomate it. The western black widow (*Latrodectus hesperus*)—relatively large with a scarlet-red hourglass on its abdomen—is an iconic image known to all. This is the female of the species, which at adulthood is actually all black (no red). Females make webs in trees and under rocks, but have also adapted all too well to human dwellings. Males remain tiny and are brightly striped; rarely are they identified as black widows. They don't make webs; instead, their lives revolve around a constant search for females. Those accounts of female black widows eating their mates immediately after engaging in spider sex are true, but more often than not males escape unharmed.

Black widows have a well-deserved reputation for being venomous; their bites frequently send victims to Urgent Care with symptoms ranging from flu-like muscle pain, sweating, and fever, to respiratory paralysis in severe cases. Bites are extremely unlikely to be lethal, but can result in painful symptoms for several days. The good news is that while the species is very common, it's also shy, unaggressive, and usually bites only defensively—if you actually put your hand on it while reaching into a dark place it's occupying, for example, or attempt to brush it off your clothing. You're only likely to see one out and about at night.

Brown widows (*L. geometricus*) are often mistaken for their more famous cousins. Unlike black widows, browns are not native to the Los Angeles basin, but are reported regularly and appear to be expanding their distribution. They prefer more exposed locations outdoors and are a bit smaller than black widows. The female's abdominal hourglass is more orange than red, or sometimes not present at all. Their bite is also less toxic, though they're still not a species you want to be bitten by. A third species, the noble false widow *(Steatoda nobilis)*, is harmless, not in the widow family at all but frequently mistaken for one: dark brown with a white, blotchy abdominal mark. These spiders were introduced worldwide from their native home in the Canary Islands, and are common in and around homes in the Los Angeles basin.

Most everyone would agree that a tarantula *(Aphonopelma spp.)* is the most dramatic manifestation of a spider, both in the imagination and in reality. Many find there to be something truly creepy about their hairy bodies, their ominously deliberate walking style, and their large and powerful jaws. Some species of tarantula are colorful, others drab; some are small and almost dainty while others are gargantuan. While they're most associated with warm places, tarantulas are found worldwide except Antarctica: an ancient and very successful group with roots in North America during the age of dinosaurs. As the continents drifted, so did tarantulas, and they proved adept at colonizing new environments from rainforests to deserts. As I walked through a Peruvian rainforest while studying wildlife there, the tarantulas I surprised on the trail would rear back on their hind legs, throwing open their front legs menacingly. The first several times, this truly unnerved me.

Several species of tarantula live in the Los Angeles basin, but they're much more likely to be seen in mountains and canyons outside. Our local species, the brown tarantula *(A. hentzi)*, is a drably colored crawler of medium size for a tarantula, albeit huge for any other spider. A few autumns ago, while driving across the Carrizo Plain a few hours north of Los Angeles, I had to stop repeatedly for all the tarantulas crossing the pavement: males on the move searching for mates. A less dramatic version of this male migration can be seen each autumn from Malibu Creek State Park to Eaton Canyon and many spots in between. Males live only a few years, whereas females may live decades. Tarantulas are slow-moving ambush predators with jaws powerful enough to crush insect prey and then consume them using regurgitated digestive fluids. Despite their fearsome appearance and reputation, most species are reluctant to bite unless harassed, and their venom's effect on people is about that of a bee sting. The approach to use if you encounter a tarantula while hiking is that of calm observation. Let the animal cross your path safely, appreciate its ancient, methodical style, and then both of you can be on your way.

The common house spider (*Parasteatoda tepidariorum*) is an introduced species that—as our name for it would suggest—is the tiny cobweb spider you often see in the corners of your ceiling. Like nearly all spiders, they're technically venomous, but their venom is intended to immobilize small insect prey that wander into their webs, and isn't known to be dangerous to people.

Wolf spiders (thousands of species worldwide, mostly in the genus *Pardosa* in our area) are among the most easily identified of our local spiders, with their characteristic high-mounted eyes, four small and two large. They occur in virtually every square inch of California except high mountain peaks, including your basement and woodpile, though likely not in your house.

They range in size from tiny to almost tarantula-like, and the largest species are often mistaken for the latter. Wolf spiders are nocturnal ambush hunters, relying on vision, stealth, and speed instead of a web to catch prey. If you shine a flashlight into your garden at night, you might see pairs of tiny, shining green dots: wolf spider eyeshine. If handled or harassed by a human, a wolf spider will bite, but beyond a bit of pain and swelling, their venom generally causes no significant medical problems.

Crab spiders, like wolf spiders, are a huge group of thousands of species (mostly *Mecaphesa spp.* in our area). They have bright yellow or white bodies, and their name speaks to the fact that they walk sideways at times, crab-style. Their eight eyes—the spider maximum, mounted front and center—aren't very good at seeing prey until it's very close, but they can detect moving objects and potential prey from a foot or more away. Though crab spiders do make and use silk, they're most often encountered while sitting on garden plants and flowers waiting to ambush prey. Like most of the spiders in Los Angeles and environs, they play a role as biological pest-control agents, eating innumerable small-insect pests that most people would rather be rid of than the spiders themselves.

Among the myriad other spiders in the Los Angeles basin, a few groups commonly seen are worth noting. Some sac spiders are native (*Cheiracanthium inclusum*) and some are introduced from Europe (*C. mildei*). They're both little, less than half an inch in size, yellowish in color, and usually seen at night walking on walls or ceilings. They're not aggressive, but do have a nasty bite when threatened or harassed.

Cellar spiders (*Pholcus spp.*) are spindly legged arachnids highly adapted to living with humans. They're mildly venomous but with such tiny fangs that it would seem impossible they could actually bite. Most often, they're mistaken for so-called "daddy longlegs" (more properly known as harvestmen, *Opiliones spp.*), which are not spiders at all, and also harmless. Cellar spiders are extremely common in cellars, basements, and garages, where they perform the admirable role of catching flies and mosquitoes.

Jumping spiders (mostly *Phidippus spp.*) are the largest spider group in Southern California with dozens of species living here, a small fraction of the thousands of species worldwide. They're usually less than half an inch in size and often colorful, featuring a palette of greens and reds with brilliantly hued jaws. They possess among the best eyesight of any of the spiders, which comes in handy when they make leaps of twenty or thirty times their body length. Jumping spiders make do without webs; they actively stalk prey in daylight and catch flies and other insects, performing the same pest-control duties of many of the spiders in your backyard.

Ground spiders are another group common in many parts of the world, with one species native to Europe that now lives throughout the western United States: the so-called mouse spider (*Scotophaeus blackwalli*). It's a very pretty little spider with smooth gray-brown hairs on its abdomen, hence its common name. Like jumping and crab spiders, ground spiders don't make webs; they hunt for a living, catching insects and other spiders by night, although they do make silk that can be used to subdue their prey. Daytime finds them secreted under logs and rocks. They're scary-looking creatures, but like most spiders, they're harmless.

Finally, trapdoor spiders (*Bothriocyrtum californicum*) are little, chunky, glossy-black spiders that resemble tarantulas without all the body hair. You can turn over rocks or logs to reveal their silk-lined burrows, and sometimes winter rains force them out. They look dangerous, with oversized jaws (really pedipalps used for manipulating food items), and can deliver a painful bite.

Of all the animals that live among us in Los Angeles suburbia, spiders are the only one that both inspires fear and revulsion and also routinely turns up in the house. If learning about something you fear makes it more comprehensible and therefore less frightening, we all ought to be reading up on spider biology. There's no more fascinating group of animals on the planet.

III.

THEIR LAST STAND

13

The (Once) Mighty Oak

Oaks are not only the largest of all native Los Angeles trees; they're also among the most important and spectacular life forms in this, or any, temperate ecosystem. People who can't tell a sycamore from an elm know when they're gazing up at an oak. Many of Southern California's oaks share the magnificent spread of enormous boughs for which the English oak of Shakespearean yore was famed. Walk across a grassy hillside dotted with huge oaks; the sheer biological bulk of the ancient behemoths almost defies belief. The weight of hardwood trees in California, comprising all species, is more than a half-billion tons. Of that weight, oaks make up a large fraction. The blue oak *(Quercus douglasi)*, of interior regions of central and Northern

California, is the most abundant oak in the state, with our own live oaks *(Q. agrifolia* and *Q. wislizeni)* close behind.

Oaks are famed for their massive bulk and great age. Not all oak species are enormous, but many reach trunk diameters of nearly ten feet, and crowns that extend more than fifty feet across. They provide shelter for everything from bears and bobcats to woodpeckers, and the vast crops of acorns they produce have fed wildlife and people for millennia. Indigenous peoples of Southern California benefited from the seasonal crops of acorns. The Tongva people and other California native peoples perfected the laborious technique of turning acorns into a highly nutritious staple diet.

From the standpoint of their own survival, one of the saving graces of our native oaks is that they are not used extensively in building. Their trunks and large limbs tend to be contorted, knobby and crooked, unlike the smooth, straight elegance of a tall pine. Most oaks have the profile of a vast umbrella, although a younger tree—less than a century old—may not yet embody that fully adult shape. Under ideal growing conditions, most oaks strive to be massive parasols.

The acorn itself is a small bit of biological beauty. Once an oak's pollen, released from myriad little flowers in the spring, secretes sperm cells and one of them fertilizes an ovule, the fertilized egg develops into an embryonic oak. These tiny seeds of a future goliath grow rapidly, each contained within a shell—the acorn—which is basically an ovary. Inside, underneath multiple layers of tissue, is the cotyledon, the embryonic leaf. Through the warm growing months, the acorn grows to accommodate the seed within, turns brown at maturity, and eventually falls. Each acorn represents the reproductive investment by the parent tree into each little propagule.

Once on the ground, the acorn lies in the deep shade of its parent. By hogging all the sunlight for many meters around, the oak's wide crown not only maximizes photosynthesis, it also minimizes competitors for that sunlight. Only shade-tolerant plants can grow in the deep shadow of a large oak. The oak's own progeny will have a tough time, since an acorn that falls only a few meters from its parental trunk might not have a shaft of light in which to grow. Most often, the huge area under a spreading oak is bare soil covered by a thick layer of dead leaves. But the goal of any tree is to spread its seeds far and wide, well beyond the edge of the canopy, in hopes of setting its progeny elsewhere. Oaks accomplish the mission by producing huge numbers of tiny acorns, protecting the seeds inside well, and making them appealing to a variety of animals to harvest. The acorns are nutrient rich, packed with protein and fat. Some animals like squirrels even bury them, doing the oak a service by planting its offspring in potential growth sites. Like many trees, oaks protect their essential products by injecting them with the byproducts of their metabolism. Tannins are one such byproduct, and they render acorns inedible by humans until they're boiled to leach out the noxious compounds.

A single large oak can produce tens of thousands of acorns in a single season. But sometimes an oak "takes some time off" and produces only a limited yield for years or more. A local population of oaks often produces a vastly larger number of acorns in a single year than the several years before and after. This effect is called mast, and while it's not entirely understood, it is most likely related to patterns of rainfall and temperature in preceding years. The phenomenon is also seen in rainforest trees in the tropics, and its impact can drive the reproductive cycles of many forest animals that depend on the trees for their sustenance.

The oak's roots, meanwhile, radiate inexorably from its trunk, eventually buckling sidewalks and retaining walls that stand in their way. They're hubs surrounding a central taproot that in most oaks dives deep into the earth, seeking out water far underground, a necessity in an arid landscape. An interdependency between oak roots and networks of soil fungi play a critical metabolic role. The roots of an oak are cloaked in mycorrhizae, a fungus that aids the oak by helping to acquire water and nutrients from the surrounding soil. The oak's mighty roots use enzymes to access the fungal layer, taking some minerals and nutrients while giving the fungus a place to make its living.

Above- and belowground, a wide variety of animals rely on oaks. Hundreds of species of insects and other invertebrates use parts of the tree to survive, whether the crown, the trunk, or the roots. Parasitic wasps lay their eggs in bizarre-looking, but quite harmless, swellings—called galls—along the twigs of oak crowns. Insects feed on developing acorns. In the Sierra foothills, black bears—and in times past, California grizzlies—bulked up their fat for winter by feasting on black oak acorns during autumn. Acorn woodpeckers not only hammer their way into oak bark in search of insects; they also harvest acorns by the hundreds and store them in "granaries" for later consumption. These oak granaries become the focus of their colonial life. Scrub jays rely on acorns and help oak trees by burying their acorns for safe storage. Jays get a nutritious food source, and oaks spread their seeds far and wide. Other jay species help oaks in other regions too, and some argue that the dispersal of jay species throughout the world has facilitated the spread of oaks to the same regions. The trees themselves provide shelter and nesting sites for myriad birds and mammals. At least one amphibian—the arboreal salamander (*Aneides lugubris*) is highly dependent on oak woodlands for its survival.

There are more than two hundred species of oaks in North America and nine large oaks in California, but only five species of large oaks occur naturally in the Los Angeles basin: the coastal and interior live oaks mentioned above, plus the canyon oak (*Q. chrysolepis*), the

Engelmann oak *(Q. engelmanni)*, and the valley oak *(Q. lobata)*. These are still present in suburbia, though some are very rare now, and all are under intense threat from developers and residents.

Coastal live oaks are the species most familiar and iconic to residents of the Los Angeles basin, with their contorted architecture, rippled gray bark, and thousands of narrow conical acorns scattered on the ground beneath. Remnant populations exist in most neighborhoods, from the west side of Los Angeles all the way into the San Gabriel Valley and beyond. The largest are likely more than three hundred years old, with a canopy spread of a hundred feet. Since that is wider than the average width of a suburban plot, it's easy to see why this magnificent tree is not beloved by realtors or non-oak-loving home buyers.

Although it's called coastal, the coastal live oak lives happily in canyons and on hillslopes more than thirty miles inland, in fiercely hot and dry summers and rainy winters. But two other very similar oaks live in the upper and more interior areas of the basin. The interior live oak is perhaps best known in the Sierra Nevada foothills, where it is replaced at higher elevations by the black oak *(Q. douglasi)*, the commonest oak in Yosemite Valley, Sequoia National Park, and elsewhere. The canyon live oak prefers cooler, moister ravines and canyons, but also lives quite well in our basin, although it may not reach the same height and spread as it would elsewhere.

My favorite oaks, ones which I've planted wherever I've lived in hopes of helping the species hang on into a future century, are Engelmann and valley oaks. Both were once common, are stunningly beautiful as adults, have storied places in the history of Southern California, and have been reduced to near extirpation in the suburbs of Los Angeles. Engelmann oaks were only recently widespread in parts of Southern California, and are even seen in the fossil record of our area. In recorded history, this majestic tree has clung to survival mainly along the coast, scattered here and there but not approaching the density the species once enjoyed in places like the San Gabriel Valley. Engelman oaks that were once important components of vast oak woodlands now stand as lonely sentinels in suburbia. Some Engelmann lovers have mapped their locations and collected their acorns in hopes of perpetuating their genetic stock. The first thing I planted when I moved into my new house was, symbolically, a baby Engelmann oak grown from a locally sourced acorn.

The valley oak is, or was, perhaps the most iconic oak in many parts of the Los Angeles basin. If some live and Engelmann oaks are large, the valley oak is a giant, reaching more than a hundred feet in height with a vast, spreading network of large boughs making a shady crown: one of the larger trees in North America. The valley oak is unlike other Southern California oaks in a couple of important ways. First, it is somewhat less drought tolerant and grows near water, or at least subsurface water. Perhaps because of its relative water dependence, when growing in optimal, moist conditions a valley oak can grow rapidly—well, rapidly for an oak—and reach its enormous dimensions more quickly than other species. It may also ultimately outlive the others; lifespans of up to six hundred years are not outrageous. Second, the valley oak is deciduous. Its lobed leaves fall in November in our area and are quickly replaced during the late winter rains. This is not a trait beloved by homeowners, nor is the valley oak's huge spreading stature or its invasive roots. This species has been felled in huge numbers in moister, flatter areas where suburban developments and agriculture now hold sway, leaving it to cling to an existence largely in drier areas that are not so conducive to its desire to grow to huge size. Of all the five big species of Southern California oak, the valley oak may be the most imperiled.

Oaks and suburbia don't get along well. Imagine a four-hundred-year-old oak that has been growing since Europeans arrived in North America, thriving on the seasonal boom and bust nature of our winter rains/summer drought ecosystem. Along comes a suburbanite who wants nothing more than an emerald green lawn and a garden of exotic plants. He dumps thousands of gallons of water on the lawn around the base of the giant oak in summer, when it has never before experienced sodden soil packing its roots. Repeat this year after year, and you have a sick oak tree. So-called oak root rot (*Armillaria mellea* and its compatriot, *Phytophthora cinnamomi*) attack the root system, eventually killing the tree. Older oaks are most vulnerable, their long adaptation to limited water and cyclical droughts upended by the lowly lawn sprinkler. More recently, other diseases have emerged. Sudden oak disease is caused by a fungus-like organism, *Phytophthora ramorum*. First reported in Central California, it's been spreading north and south since.

But destruction of the vast stands of old California oaks began before suburbanization. The early ranches of the Spanish era spelled doom. Even when large old trees themselves were not cut down, live-stock and farming tools destroyed young trees, ensuring that this generation of the region's giant oaks would be the last. Logging of oaks as fuel wood was lucrative and a bustling business. Later, new colonists of California with eyes for profit demolished oak woodlands in order to plant citrus orchards, for which the valleys became famous. Finally, as suburban subdivisions grew, developers felled oaks by the thousands to make ways for houses, streets, and nonnative exotic plants. Home buyers paying premium prices for even the more modest homes in our area don't appreciate being told they can't cut down the old oak in the backyard, its limbs spanning the entire property, in order to install the swimming pool of their dreams.

A few years ago, severe winds rushed down the canyons of the San Gabriels and wrought arboreal devastation to the Pasadena area, downing more than a thousand trees. Some were ancient oaks. The natural disaster was compounded by human eco-crime: many homeowners took advantage of all the downed trees to cut down their healthy large oaks, skirting the strict city ordinances that regulate pruning oaks and levee hefty fines on those who cut them down without good reason. They claimed the winds had done them in, that their chainsawing was just cleanup. When I was house shopping shortly thereafter, I read online realtor advertisements that said "Great yard! Wonderful lawn, fruit trees, and *No Oaks*!"

More oaks fall every year during winter storms, often weakened by sprinkler-softened soil and a host of fungal and bacterial infections. Some cities have begun planting young oaks, usually coast live oaks, on curb strips, in hopes the trees will someday provide leafy bowers over the streets, bringing a semblance of environmental normality back to the suburbs. But it will take well over a hundred years for these trees to begin to mature, and meanwhile the older oaks in the same cities will continue to die, or fall, or be cut down illegally. The pace of death of the old oaks, and the failure to plant new ones for so many decades, means that even with the best replanting efforts, the suburbs of Los Angeles will see decades with very few adult oak trees.

Oaks are not the only native trees in the suburban forest of our landscape, but they are the most vulnerable. The beautiful western sycamore *(Platanus racemosa)*, resplendent with a trunk of palomino white and brown, grows rapidly enough to populate areas from which its ancestors were felled long ago. Same for the California black walnut *(Juglans californica)* and California bay laurel *(Umbellularia californica)*, local treasures that often cohabitate with oaks in our local canyons and valleys. Like oaks, both species have been felled in large numbers, but unlike oaks, they grow rapidly to large size when given half a chance to survive.

Oaks have been the crux of a California ecosystem of plants and animals for millennia. Visit an area of ancient oaks today and search for seedling and young oaks. They are hard to find. Agriculture, invasive plants, livestock, burgeoning deer populations and fire suppression in fire-adapted ecosystems have especially ravaged the trees that are less than a hundred or so years old. There is, in biological parlance, no recruitment.

With California's population reaching forty million, and half of that population living in the Los Angeles basin, there is increasingly little room for ecosystems dominated by enormous, spreading trees. Preserving the scattered remnants in suburbia is a last hope, and it won't be easily achieved. We can plant new generations of oaks, remove the invasive plants around them, and protect the land from livestock and deer. But such habitat restoration is a laborious, slow, and sometimes expensive process, often on land sought by developers. Preserving the healthy, ancient stands of oaks that remain, and the land around them, is better than trying to reconvert already-developed areas to their former natural state. If we can manage that, we will preserve a Los Angeles in which a semblance of balance between humanity and Nature continues to exist, for the benefit of all of us.

14

Silent Suburbia

It's a lovely April morning in Pasadena, and I'm at work in my home office, a converted garden shed seventy-five feet behind my house. A wren scrambles, flits, and hops among the branches of a bay laurel tree almost within arm's reach of my office door. A bulbul warbles a strikingly robin-like song from the telephone line above, a few feet from which a little screech owl was perched late last night. The air is abuzz with hummingbirds jousting with one another at the sugar water feeder, and a bevy of band-tailed pigeons has alighted to feed on fallen bird seed, scattering a dozen mourning doves in the process. Jays and finches spray birdseed around as they gobble a morning meal. A lovely red-shouldered hawk sits high atop a pine tree in my neighbor's yard. The hawk is not as magnificent as the peregrine falcon that frequented the tree before my neighbor wantonly chopped off its crown, but at least he was the beneficiary of the tree mutilation. All in all, it's a wonderful suburban wildlife experience.

In my postage stamp–sized backyard in South Pasadena, a plot of grass and ancient trees and native plantings no more than three thousand square feet, I saw nearly one hundred species of birds over a twenty-year period. Birds are drawn to a birdbath and several feeders full of seed and suet and sugar water, and to greenery planted with them in mind: trees that produce berries favored by orioles; flowering bushes that are hummingbird favorites. Over that twenty-year period, suet stuck in tree bark drew four different species of woodpeckers.

My home office gives me a dawn-to-dusk view of these avian comings and goings. The species I've seen include nonnative parrots and peafowl, which a purist birdwatcher wouldn't count. Red-whiskered bulbuls *(Pycnonotus jocasus)*, escaped cage birds from Southeast Asia, are common breeding residents in the Pasadena area, but not officially established in North America. Other bird species have flown over my yard, like turkey vultures *(Cathartes aura)* and great blue herons *(Ardea herodias)*. Many of my visitors are likely migrating up or down the west coast when they spot my little yard—or rather hear the commotion of regular bird residents—and alight to see what all the fuss is about. They discover food that many local backyards lack, and then stay a few hours before continuing their journey. Migrants like Nashville *(Leiothlypis ruficapilla)* and Townsend's *(Setophaga townsendi)* warblers, and warbling vireos *(Vireo gilvus)*, turn up occasionally. Some hang around for weeks, especially in winter when finding a food source can delay or even interrupt their migration. I've had lengthy winter visits from summer *(Piranga rubra)* and western *(P. ludoviciana)* tanagers, fox *(Passerella iliaca)* and chipping *(Spizella passerina)* sparrows, rose-breasted grosbeaks *(Pheucticus ludovicianus)*, and cedar waxwings *(Bombycilla cedrorum)*. During occasional winters when little pine siskins *(Spinus pinus)* flood out of the mountains and into our backyards, thirty or more at a time clamber over the feeders.

Other visitors are likely blown off course or just lost. A beautiful young male scarlet tanager, rarely seen in Los Angeles County, was caught by a cat in my backyard. A phainopepla *(Phainopepla nitens)*—a desert species—flapped around my yard after a storm. Birders have a fanatical ethic about rare species that show up. They will drive or even fly for hours in hopes of seeing some wayward bird lost on its intended migration. A Siberian bluethroat *(Luscinia svecica)* turns up in a city park in Santa Monica and throngs of birders draped in binoculars and telephoto lenses show up the next day, eager to tick off a new species on their life lists. The poor avian visitor sitting in the tree in front of them is exhausted from its travails, and likely doomed to die before finding the correct course to wherever it intended to go. I'm a fairly avid birder with a global life list in the thousands, and I consider birding a great pastime—it connects one with the natural world, even in an urban landscape. Birding grows in popularity every year, and the billions of dollars spent by birders on equipment, ecotours, and the like have created an incentive for many communities to preserve their biodiversity rather than plow it under farm fields or shopping malls. But I can't bring myself to chase rarities; you're basically obsessing over your list, and a soon-to-be-dead feathered creature is just a prop.

The Los Angeles basin offers a wide diversity of habitats, from the coast and the ocean itself to the sea-facing moister valleys, to the drier, hotter foothills and plains, and up to tree-line elevations in some of the local surrounding mountains. It's no wonder that our bird fauna is equally diverse. More than three hundred species have been recorded in the Los Angeles basin alone. And because we're near the coast, we're in the path of migrants moving north or south in spring and fall. As a large suburban area in a Mediterranean climate, we offer favorable conditions for all manner of nonnative birds that are either released by people or find their own way here.

Why do some birds thrive in suburbia while others decline or disappear? Most animal species have adapted over millennia to a narrow range of habitat requirements. They need a particular diet or a specialized nesting spot or both. Many Angelenos believe their neighborhood is full of birds because they hear birds chattering in the morning and see them flying all day long. In a sense, they're correct. There are large bird populations in Los Angeles when you don't consider which species. Backyards are full of house finches *(Haemorbous mexicanus)*, northern mockingbirds *(Mimus polyglottos)*, scrub jays *(Aphelocoma californica)*, crows *(Corvus brachyrhynchos)*, and if you put out the right feeders, lesser goldfinches *(Spinus psaltria)* and various hummingbirds too. House finches, crows, and mockers are great examples of what biologists call habitat generalists; they're biologically lucky enough to be adaptable to a variety of habitats, including this weirdly manmade one. Habitat generalists are sometimes called weed species, because they tend to establish themselves everywhere. Coyotes, pigeons, rats, many squirrel species: all weed species. Some weed species rely on humans to facilitate their spread. The populations of coyotes and ravens in the desert outside Los Angeles are larger than they've ever been, largely because those species follow the growth and spread of our towns and cities. Cities need trash disposal, and landfills become superfood locales for some of these highly adaptable animals.

There is no question that suburbanization has increased

populations of a few species, mainly those that are not only generalists but also favor open park-like environments as opposed to chaparral or dense forest. In the eastern United States, robins are everywhere, thriving in open grassy areas with patches of trees nearby, as the suburbs provide. Same for mockingbirds in our area. Bird feeders have dramatically changed the habits of some species. We've already seen the altered and expanded distribution of some hummingbirds, the result of orchards, suburban flower gardens, and omnipresent sugar water feeders. But other species have boomed as well, even as most have declined. The band-tailed pigeon (*Patagioenas fasciata*) is a stunning, big dove related to the rock dove (*Columba livia*) and reminiscent of some of Europe's large wood pigeons. Band-tailed pigeons are mountain birds of pine forests, historically flocking down to the valleys and plains only in winter in search of food when the mountains are snowbound and food is scarce. Today they are ubiquitous birds of suburbia, seen most often flying overhead in small flocks, but also making the rounds of backyard feeders. Years ago, I set out a hanging tray of bird seed, which quickly attracted hordes of mourning doves, and eventually became a way station for ten to twenty band-tailed pigeons each day too.

Not all birds that become established in suburbia thrive long-term. When I moved to Southern California in the early 1990s, Asian spotted doves (*Spilopelia chinensis*) were among the exotic birds that appeared in my backyard every day. It's been a long time since I've spotted one now; the reasons for their decline are not well understood. Eurasian collared doves (*Streptopelia decaocto*) have meanwhile become more common. House sparrows (*Passer domesticus*), one of the prime examples of bird introductions gone wrong, were brought from Europe a century and a half ago, became established on the East Coast, spread west rapidly, and took over many suburban neighborhoods. But here in California they face competition from the widespread house finch, itself a beneficiary of backyard feeders. These days in the Pasadena area, house finches outnumber house sparrows by an order of magnitude.

Some success stories for birds in Los Angeles suburbia don't involve invasive species. To my eye at least, there are more western bluebirds *(Sialia mexicana)* in our area today than there were twenty years ago, and they turn up in a wide variety of habitats, including the suburbs. Lesser goldfinches, always the most common of the three goldfinch species that live in the Los Angeles basin, seem more ubiquitous than ever, likely due to the popularity of feeders stocked with their preferred thistle seeds. The same is true for hummingbirds and all those sugar-water feeders.

But for every goldfinch or Allen's hummingbird, there's a bird species threatened by suburban spread. As big oak trees disappear, Nuttall's woodpeckers *(Picoides nuttallii)* lose their main Southern California habitat. Barred white and black, with males sporting a red cockade, these are lovely little birds similar in appearance to the much more widespread downy woodpecker *(P. pubescens)*.

The disastrous and precipitous decline in bird populations in North America is well documented. The decline over the past few decades is in the billions. If you go for a walk in a canyon on a spring morning, you won't notice the decline, because the birds are out and about and singing. But the data are real. In the eastern US, some of the most common migrant warblers of a generation ago have been reduced by 80 to 95 percent. Authors of bird surveys expected to find that while birds declined dramatically in forests, grasslands, and wetlands, populations of other birds increased in suburbia, those species well adapted to humanity's presence. But they found no such thing. Instead, even the most common species—the finches, sparrows, and blackbirds whose flocks seem to fill our suburban lives, have declined by the hundreds of millions. Radar data, which show not only storm systems but huge migrating nighttime bird flocks, showed a more than 10 percent overall decline in just the past decade.

The causes of the decline are mostly obvious, though the scale of each threat can be debated. There is no question that habitat loss is the elephant in the room. Loss of natural habitat usually means conversion of that habitat to an environment uninhabitable for most bird species adapted to live there—like turning a riparian canyon of oaks and sycamores and native plants into a hillside housing subdivision of heavily watered lawns, eucalyptus trees, and palms. Few homeowners consider their well-tended lots to be degraded habitat, but from a natural standpoint, that is exactly what they are.

Pesticides are an enormous killer of songbirds. Neonicotinoids are pesticides that often coat commercially grown plant seeds, functioning as an appetite suppressant. During spring migration, when birds heading north stop to feed, newly planted seeds laden with chemicals cause them to stop feeding, rendering them unable to resume their migration to breeding grounds. Neonicotinoids have long been known to destroy honeybee populations; the link to songbird deaths was only established more recently. Grassland seed-eating birds have been particularly hard-hit, declining 4 percent annually in recent years, with pesticides much to blame.

The two greatest threats to our bird populations in suburbia come from unexpected and underappreciated causes. First is our loveable, predatory tabby cats. As I described earlier, the combined effect of more than one hundred million domestic cats, both feral and owned, roaming our landscape equates to the deaths of two billion birds annually. Many studies across nations—the US, Canada, the UK, Australia, and elsewhere—have shown conclusively that house cats wreak devastation on bird populations. They are capable of driving entire species to extinction; in fact, they have likely already done so many times. If there were one threat to the survival of our songbirds that we could lessen, it would be the prevalence of both cats living with humans that are allowed to roam and hunt, and the millions of feral cats that live by preying on small animals. Generations after we woke up to the problem of pollution and habitat loss, we woke up to the sad reality that our beloved furry pets are a serious and preventable cause of bird mortality.

A second key threat to suburban birds, of even greater and more widespread impact, is the devastation of native insects upon which the vast majority of native songbirds depend. Insect ecologist Douglas Tallamy's work showed that insect populations are smaller in landscapes of exotic plants than native ones. His research team also showed that songbirds nest mainly in backyards with native plants, at least in the eastern United States. Desirée Narango showed that chickadees in an eastern wooded suburb search for insects on native plants nearly 90 percent of the time. Yards with mostly exotic plants had fewer chickadees, and those that did nest produced fewer eggs per nest. We know that one pair of songbirds may require thousands of insects in a single nesting season to feed their young. The inescapable implication of such research is that replacing native plants with exotics creates a landscape depauperate in essential links in the food chain needed to sustain native birds and perhaps mammals. Combine this with predation on songbirds by house cats and you have a genuine environmental apocalypse, masked by the constant planting of more exotic trees and plants. Solutions are obvious but not easily achieved, but controlling our feral cat population and planting more native plants could go a long way toward restoring some ecological balance.

15

Live Forever . . .
to Be Poached

Live forevers (*Dudleya spp.*) are some of Southern California's most iconic plants. The eponym is born of the plant's rugged ability to grow in inhospitable places, thriving impossibly just above the surf line on vertical cliffs, or in shadows on scalding arid slopes. Live forevers are succulents, and many of the two dozen species in California closely resemble the nonnative succulents sold in Home Depots and Targets across North America. But *Dudleyas* are native plants, and they are uniquely lovely succulents that dot our landscape: inconspicuous most of the year but transformed into showstoppers in early spring, when colorful, long flower stalks burst forth from the leafy rosettes. Most consist of a symmetrical whorl of leathery leaves, perfect for surviving lengthy droughts. At least one, the fingertips live forever (D. edulis) takes on more alien dimensions, long and tubular. Live forevers also function as major hummingbird plants—their long flower stalks attracting the pollinators—and their toughness allows them to grow in places where other flowering plants can't, like arid cliffs and rocky shorelines. Dudleyas are named for William Dudley, a late nineteenth- and early twentieth-century Stanford University botanist after whom many plants are named, and who likely never envisioned his special genus of succulents becoming the stuff of which smuggling legends are made.

Only the perimeters of the Los Angeles basin are home to live forevers. They grow on the canyon walls of the San Gabriel Mountains, clinging to crevices at eye level along hiking trails. Driving south on the 101 Freeway into the San Fernando Valley, the wall of the roadcut known as the Camarillo Grade is dotted with the widespread lance-leaf live forever, D. lanceolata. Take a boat to the Channel Islands and you may see live forevers on seaside cliffs there too. In fact, one of the rarest of the Dudleyas—and many are nearly extinct in the wild due to their popularity in the legal and illegal plant trade—is the Santa Barbara Island live forever, D. traskiae, which grows in only a few patches of rocky ground on remote, tiny Santa Barbara Island. One of the most beautiful of the group, the thick-leafed Cedros Island live forever (D. pachyphytum) grew only on rocky Cedros Island in the Gulf of California, where it grows no more, having been collected out of existence. Another, D. stolonifera, lives in a few scattered locations across Orange County, the precise locales carefully guarded by botanists lest an army of collectors and smugglers descend upon them.

Most of the live forevers that occur in the mountains rimming the Los Angeles basin are threatened with extinction. More than half of California's species are considered rare. Listing them as Threatened with Extinction at the state level, or using the federal Endangered Species Act to gain them legally protected status, does remarkably little in many cases to assure their future. Endangered plants growing on private land are often bulldozed or built over by landowners, federally protected status notwithstanding. And many live forevers have tiny distributions—in some cases just a few clusters of plants scattered over a few miles or less.

The San Gabriel Mountains live forever is my local live forever and among the rarest of all *Dudleyas*: a dainty succulent found in just a few scattered locations in the mountains right behind my house, the whole population of the species comprising fewer than a thousand plants. There are few enough plants that a careless off-trail hiker could unintentionally stamp out a measurable fraction of the species. The saving grace may be that the canyons in which it clings precariously to existence are all located on federally protected land, the beautiful Angeles National Forest.

There is a sinister urge buried deep in human nature. We treasure the rarest things and can't find beauty in the commonest. Our desire to acquire the rarities finds its most pernicious manifestation in the global trade in endangered plants and animals. Like craving a rare edition for a stamp collection, the urge to buy, collect, or steal the rarest orchid, or parrot, or turtle has vacuumed many species from the surface of the Earth. In my work with endangered animals, I've encountered tortoises that bring upwards of $100,000 for one adult female on the global black market. There are parrots that sell for much more than that. The closer a species draws to extinction, the greater its trophy status and the more astronomical its price, incentivizing theft. This horrific dynamic is one of the perversions of human behavior that we conservationists confront while trying to preserve the planet's biodiversity.

This hunger for rare exotics most heavily impacts the developing world, where many of the rarest plants and animals live. But plant and animal poaching happens in the United States too. Saguaros that took a century to reach a couple of meters tall are dug from a stunning desert landscape to give somebody's Tucson front yard the look they wanted. The rarest turtles, parrots, and cacti are smuggled from the developing world to the US, Europe, and especially China to supply a demand for exotic pets and house plants.

And unfortunately, the plant craze includes one of the hottest new houseplants in East Asia: the live forever. They are known as "fat plants" in Asia for their robust water-storing leaves. *Dudleyas*, which sell for $50 or so on the Asian plant trade, are well worth the risk of capture for the poacher, given that a large haul may bring him hundreds of thousands of dollars. As a result, *Dudleyas* are being carved off rocky surfaces by the thousands and smuggled, often via the US Postal Service, to Asia in unmarked boxes. Because they're tough and small and drought tolerant, poachers can cut off their shallow root systems, ship them stacked like oranges, and make a tidy profit. In one recent escapade, poachers of more than 3,700 live forevers valued at $600,000 were apprehended in the process of obtaining fraudulent shipping papers to mail the plants to South Korea.

Online, you will find many species of *Dudleya* for sale, including the rarest. These are often the progeny of plants that were smuggled from California to Asia, where the collectors and cultivators are now offering to sell them back to live forever lovers in the land from which they were stolen. When a bust is made, the plants are sometimes replanted in the area from which they were poached, which is labor-intensive, and unless care is taken to put them in remote areas, they're likely to be located and poached again.

The poaching of wildlife and plants has been going for centuries. When a fad takes hold, the prices go up and the poaching is highly profitable, creating a gold rush effect. The extirpation of some of the Mexican species by poaching may have led others to turn to Southern California species as substitutes. There is bitter irony in plants called live forevers being at risk of extinction. Even while gardeners the world over fuss over their succulent gardens, in awe of the natural geometry of each plant, the importance of the plant to its ecosystem is often ignored. *Dudleyas* tend to be inconspicuous, a cluster of gray-green leaves on a dusty cliff, and when a species is gone it is missed by only the more hardcore Nature lovers and hikers who appreciate what has been lost. But that ethic is a dangerously slippery slope. Today *Dudleyas* are poached; tomorrow it may be any number of other irreplaceable species. Each generation grows up accustomed to the scope of Nature that surrounds it. As the baseline of biodiversity shifts downward, we will end up with a Southern California that is not only a strange mosaic of the native and the invasive, but also a depauperate landscape that an earlier generation would be hard pressed to recognize, and that a future generation may be hard pressed to enjoy.

16

Pollinators on Life Support

Take a stroll through a Southern California fruit orchard in spring. The trees are having sex. The air is full of honeybees, humming from flower to flower, tree to tree. They spend the night in bee boxes that have been trucked here, enabling the orchard owners to get their almonds or apples or citrus growing. Then the bees will head farther north for apple blossom season, before striking out across the United States to hit the East Coast in summer. They'll do berry season in New England, and then the trucks will turn around and head back toward Southern California for autumn and winter. The bees, evolved over fifty million years to pollinate the flowers of a few species in the same place throughout their lives, are kept in a perpetual state of jet lag and disorientation. Constant travel between seasons, climates, and time zones leaves them thoroughly stressed. But we count on them to pollinate billions of dollars' worth of crops each year in California alone. They are, from a human standpoint, perhaps the most indispensable component of the hollow nonnative ecosystem we have built.

The honeybee that we are all familiar with is actually a genetic mixture of several honeybee species from Europe, the Mediterranean, and Africa that interbreed. North America has no native honeybees; they were introduced to North America at the time of the earliest European colonists in the 1600s, and ever since have played a critical role in cultivation of some of our most important foods.

The Central Valley, beginning just north of the Los Angeles basin, is one of the world's most productive agricultural areas. Nearly three-quarters of all the domestic plant crops grown worldwide and in California depend on honeybees for their pollination. Almonds, walnuts, avocados, oranges, lemons, grapefruits, tangerines, and assorted other tree fruits rely entirely on bees for reproduction and survival. In one almond orchard alone, there might be hundreds of bee boxes, each one generating nearly two thousand dollars' worth of almonds. Wild crops were pollinated by native American bees for millennia, and many still are. But imported European honeybees (*Apis mellifera*) are the mainstay of the entire agroindustry of North America. The majority of California's agricultural industry depends on pollinators, and is valued at more than $12 billion annually.

Bees evolved from ancient wasps more than a hundred million years ago, when their lineage split from carnivorous wasps in order to take advantage of a younger Earth's new food resources: pollen and nectar from emerging flowering plants. As with wasps, there are solitary species as well as many highly social species. And as with other social insects, there's a queen that overwinters with at least part of the colony. Most social bees live in colonies in which some members are caregivers for offspring. They stock a nest with pollen to feed their larvae, and with nectar mostly for themselves. Most solitary bees stock individual nest cells with all the nutrients the young will need to mature.

As we saw with butterflies and birds, generalist bee species that can utilize a variety of plants and habitats in Los Angeles tend to be at a far lower risk of extinction than specialist species that require just one or two plant species for their survival. Most American bumblebees, for example, feed from a variety of flower species from spring to autumn. But many bee species require one or two particular plants for their existence. Even the seasonal activity cycles of specialist bees are synchronized with the flowering seasons of their host plants. The symbiosis works well until we remove their host plants through habitat destruction, leaving the bees with nothing to show for their tireless search for pollen.

The search for nectar is all-consuming for bees during the warmer months; it's the basis of their diet and the raw material from which honey is made. From a plant's perspective, pollen is the reproductive material that must be transferred to other plants, and sweet nectar is the lure that attracts the bees as vectors of pollen. Bees use pollen in critical nutritional ways too; it is food for the queen and is mixed with nectar to feed larvae. Pollen baskets adorn the hind legs of both honeybees and bumblebees. Their tiny flight muscles generate body heat, and they need to fuel their intense activity by finding huge numbers of flowers each day.

Bees find their fuel through what biologists call optimal foraging. They make route choices based on the maximum expected caloric return for the caloric energy expended. Anything less than maximum efficiency would waste precious energy need for survival and reproduction. When foraging, some routes are more efficient than others and some flowers are richer in their sugary reward. In some flowering plants, the bottom-most flowers are older and contain more nectar; bees tend to hit them first and ignore those at the top that are less sugar rich. Experience counts; the more trips a bee makes to a flower patch, the higher its rate of pollen collection and the greater the bounty collected. Many studies have found that as the pollen yield from a field of flowers declines over a season, bees spend less and less time there. As houses replace meadows and crops replace wildflowers, pollen and nectar sources are fewer and farther between, and finding food gets ever more difficult for wild bees.

Pollinators are in terrible trouble in Southern California and world-wide. The threats to their survival are many, and scientists don't agree on which are the most critical. Insecticides, parasites like bee mites, and the constant movement of bee colonies around the country to pollinate various crops, regardless of distance and season: all of these stressors leave bees disease prone. When you spray pesticides on your flowering plants or inject pesticidal chemicals into the soil, it ends up in honeybees, either directly on their bodies or through the pollen that they gather. If the pesticide exposure is intense, it's lethal to the bee. If the exposure is less than lethal, the bee will bring the toxin back to its hive and contaminate the colony. Moreover, when multiple pesticides are in use—as is frequent in agricultural areas—the synergy of the chemicals can generate a terribly lethal effect that may kill not only bees but also other wildlife.

Since the mid-2000s, honeybees have been decimated by disease in some areas. Sometimes they're covered with a white film—fungicide residue. Colony collapse disorder, in which honeybees turn up dead or blackened and sickly, has spread like wildfire and now endangers entire apiaries and the livelihood of beekeepers. Fungicide doesn't kill the bees outright; they carry it back to their hive and a couple of weeks later, bees die en masse. Those that survive are more liable to die of other diseases afterward. Pesticides, on the other hand, are systemic and end up in every part of a tree, remaining on or in the soil for years. They hit bees' nervous systems like a cruise missile, leaving whole colonies dead or dying. Pesticide companies in the US adamantly deny their products have anything to do with the massive die-off of bees nationwide, but it's easy to see they are a major culprit. Europeans have banned the main pesticides used in the United States, and that continent is no longer experiencing our scale of honeybee colony collapse.

Other culprits contribute to honeybee die-off as well. Varroa mites, tiny disc-shaped parasites that bite bees and transmit a virus to them, have devastated some honeybee colonies in the United States and around the world. Climate scientists think climate change is affecting bees by changing the timing of the seasons and making it easier for the parasitic mites to survive the long winters. Bee keeping has crashed in North America, with more and more honey coming from other countries, especially China and the European Union. There are currently half as many bee colonies in the United States as there were fifty years ago. In some years, beekeepers lost huge portions of their colonies due to the still-mysterious colony collapse disorder, to the point that in some states half the honeybee population disappeared.

Cell phone signals may disorient bees, causing them to fly irregular paths to flowers and waste precious time and energy. The more the honeybees are trucked here and there and expected to perform like pollinating automatons, the more mortality the colonies experience. Stress, parasites, and pesticides have combined to create a bee pandemic. Whatever the causes, bee populations are in steep decline, and the factors causing declines in introduced European honeybees also cause die-offs of native bees. Honeybees have been slowly driving native bees toward extinction since the nonnatives were brought to North America hundreds of years ago. The more recent stressors may simply be accelerating a decline that was already in motion.

However severe the problems facing honeybees, they are human-managed as any very valuable domesticated livestock or crop would be, and so their plight is well-documented and much attention has been paid to solutions. Meanwhile, Southern California is home to more than a thousand species of native bees, pollinating our Southern California plants for eons before the European honeybees arrived. In many cases, they still do a better job of it. Most native bees are solitary, unlike the intensely social and highly visible European honeybee. Some are tiny and inconspicuous, while others are giants, like bumblebees. Many nest singly in soil or in cavities in wood, versus in bustling, noisy hives. Little mining bees (family Andrenidae) have nested in my garden soil for years, their perforations dotting dry areas. They pollinate many flowers that honeybees can't. Indeed, a study by Gordon Frankie and colleagues in California urban gardens found that the vast majority of garden pollinators were native bees, not the more easily observed European honeybees. Casual observers might mistake some native bees for honeybees. The yellow-faced bumble bee *(Bombus vosnesenskii)* and California bumblebee *(Bombus californicus)* are often seen moving slowly from flower to flower: both renowned pollinators of tomato crops in our region. Other species, like the huge black valley carpenter bee *(Xylocopa varipuncta)* cruise slowly and noisily through a backyard, pollinating flowers alongside the nonnative honeybees.

European honeybees are vital to pollinating our fruit tree orchards, and to a lesser extent, our flower gardens. But many crops, from cherries to cranberries to pumpkins, are more effectively and eagerly pollinated by native bees. Blueberries in the eastern United States rely on the southeastern blueberry bee (*Habropoda laboriosa*) for pollination; one blueberry bee can pollinate flowers that produce several thousand ripe blueberries.

Bumblebees of the genus *Bombus* are among the most iconic of all bees, and are perhaps in the most trouble. There are more than twenty species of bumblebees in California. Unlike smaller native bees in Southern California that face harsh competition from invasive bees, bumblebees have virtually no invasive bumblebees to contend with. However, in every agricultural area surrounding Los Angeles, bumblebees are in decline from the pervasive use of insecticides. A study in England found that urban bumblebee populations are in better shape than those in more rural areas, perhaps because the city and suburban bees cope better with insecticide use.

As pollinators, native bees are critical for the survival and reproduction of more plant species in Southern California and elsewhere than European honeybees are. And they are exposed to toxic pesticides just as introduced honeybees are. Our reliance on one bee species—the European honeybee—is dangerous to the bees themselves and also to our food supply. Take away honeybees and much of our fruit and vegetable supply—and, indirectly, even our dairy supply—collapses.

Can anything be done to prevent bee extinction? We can at least mitigate some of the threats. Conservation and beekeeping organizations both have a deep interest in monitoring the status and health of managed and wild bee populations worldwide. Organizations in multiple countries have funded efforts to prevent further bee declines by studying how environmental contaminants affect bee DNA and hurt bee populations. The US Environmental Protection Agency is following the European Union by removing pesticides that contain neonicotinoids, which are highly toxic to bees, from the market.

On a more local level, we can all help both managed and wild bee populations in our own yards. Planting nectar-rich flowers and other plants will of course benefit many pollinators. Some native bees will use wooden nest boxes with holes drilled into them. Providing a water source like a birdbath or guzzler helps too. Of course, one important thing you can do is stop applying pesticides to your vegetables or flowers. We've already seen how sterile a green turf lawn is from an insect perspective. Planting a "bee lawn"—grass seed mixes that are full of wildflowers—turns a monolithic lawn into an attractively diverse mix of green grass and fields of flowers that helps local bee populations and a whole community of other insects, thereby ultimately supporting native plants and other animals.

Bees need help on a grand scale to survive the perils of habitat loss, toxins, parasites, and other human-induced stressors. Each of us can play a role in their survival by changing the way we manage the tiny ecosystem we call our backyard.

IV.

BACKYARD VISITORS

17

Aerial Hunters
in the Backyard

The evening routine began with the big raptor alighting in the top of our neighbors' towering pine tree. The first time it arrived, I ran for the binoculars, not trusting my eyes that a peregrine falcon *(Falco peregrinus)* had landed in suburban South Pasadena. But a peregrine it was: black cowl, white cheeks and breast, and striking gray-blue mantle. Nearly every sunset, the falcon sat atop that pine with a mourning dove clutched in its talons, and proceeded to rip the dove apart while we sat far below on our deck. The two of us, bird of prey and hungry human family, shared dinnertime, with downy dove feathers wafting down around us as we ate. Presumably, the peregrine hunted all over the area by day, when we rarely saw it. By late afternoon it was ready to settle in for the night, preferably with a meal in tow. The peregrine was a daily presence until the day our neighbor brought in a work crew to top the pine tree. Despite our appeals, the top twenty or so feet of the tree was buzz-sawed off, and the falcon never returned. Afterward the pine became a perch for ravens *(Corvus corax)* or an occasional red-shouldered hawk *(Buteo lineatus)*, but nary a falcon.

Birds of prey are symbols of American wildness—cue the bald eagle soaring overhead with snow-capped mountains in the distance—but in fact many suburban and even urban areas have raptor populations. After eggshell-destroying DDT and other pesticides were banned in the 1960s, fish-eating ospreys *(Pandion haliaetus)* rebounded to become fixtures of coastal areas around the United States. Bald eagles *(Haliaeetus leucocephalus)* nest in urban parks, and peregrines have decided skyscrapers are as good for nesting as natural cliffs, laying their eggs on ledges outside the fortieth floors of downtown buildings. Many other species have suffered from urbanization, but a few have not only survived in the face of civilization, but also thrived.

In suburban Los Angeles, a rich diversity of raptors cruise our skies by day, and another cast of characters take over by night. At least six raptor species reside in and around our neighborhoods, with several more migrating through twice a year or living just beyond suburbia in the mountains and seacoast that surround us. Add in the nocturnal owls, which number three common species plus a few more that are rare or live only in local mountains, and that's a plethora of raptor biodiversity. A peregrine in the backyard is a rare and special thing, but a red-tailed hawk soaring over Dodger

Stadium or perched above a freeway sign in downtown Los Angeles is a spectacular everyday sight.

Red-tailed hawks *(Buteo jamaicensis)* are the most common and most observed large American raptors. They number in the millions in North America and have taken up residence in many American cities. Manhattan may have up to twenty nesting pairs, some of which have photo blogs devoted to them. Like many hawk species, red-tails are highly variable in color. A red-tail perched in a distant tree can be almost black, almost white, or any variation of brown and white patterning in between, with an eponymous red-orange tail. They're mammal eaters, soaring or perching above grassy areas from Alaska to Latin America to spot prey before diving onto it. Unlike peregrines, which may nest on the bare concrete ledges of skyscrapers, red-tails most often make their nests of twigs and leafy branches in treetops or atop similar platforms; the tallest tree in the area is a likely locale. Parents take shifts sitting on the eggs and then bringing torn-up rodents, squirrels, and the like to feed their chicks. A recent survey tallied at least twenty active nests within a few miles of Griffith Park. That includes habitat ranging from wooded ravines to grassy plains to urban streets. The survey found that red-tail nests were actually more abundant in nonnative trees and outside the forested confines of the park itself.

Red-shouldered hawks *(Buteo lineatus)*, the other chunky-bodied raptors seen in Los Angeles suburbia, are not as common as red-tails. They're a bit smaller than red-tails, and less conspicuous even where they're common. You might spot their rust-colored epaulettes, but you'll more likely note the black and white bands on their tail that identify them best. I've found them sitting quietly in tall trees in my yards, scanning the ground for an unwary rodent or lizard no doubt. Other large-bodied hawks make occasional appearances in our area;

beautiful Swainson's hawks *(Buteo swainsoni)* show off their dark chestnut plumage while migrating over Los Angeles in spring and fall, sometimes in startlingly large numbers.

While red-tailed and red-shouldered hawks are most often seen flying or perched far overhead, Los Angeles suburbia has smaller raptors that literally live among us. I have been fond of Cooper's hawks *(Accipiter cooperii)* ever since moving to Southern California. In the eastern United States, a Cooper's sighting is a noteworthy event. Here in LA, Cooper's are downright common; in the same survey of raptor nests in which red-tailed nests were most prevalent, Cooper's came in second. Anyone who lives near a tall tree will at some point see a Cooper's hawk in it—either swooping in to attack a dove or perched quietly in hopes of grabbing an unsuspecting bird underneath. Cooper's hawks are bird eaters, and brazen predators. They attack slower birds in the vicinity of a bird feeder, diving to make a kill right in front of a coffee-drinking suburbanite enjoying a quiet morning on the back deck. I've seen Cooper's hawks perched calmly on my porch chairs, my birdbath, and on the fence right outside my office window.

Coopers hawks are *Accipiters*—having more elongated, slender bodies than the *Buteo* group that includes red-tails and red-shoulders and Swainson's. Cooper's hawks share our LA ecosystem with a very similar but smaller *Accipiter*, the sharp-shinned hawk *(Accipiter striatus)*. Sharpies are the common small-bird-eating hawk in much of the United States, but here in Southern California they seem to live in the shadow of their larger Cooper's kin. They're not easily distinguished from Cooper's by a novice birder; because the females of most hawk species are larger, a female sharpie and a male Cooper's are very similar in size. With some practice, one can distinguish the sharpie's squared-off tail from the rounded tip of the Cooper's tail.

And the sharp-shinned is more likely to show up as a spring or fall migrant, or a winter visitor, rather than residing in our area year-round like most Cooper's.

We are fortunate to have raptors like Cooper's and sharp-shinned hawks in our backyards. They prey largely on small birds that have benefited enormously from bird feeders, like mourning doves. We may be sympathetic to their gentle prey species, but predators have to eat too, and the dignity and grace of these creatures are no less than their prey's. Cooper's and sharp-shinned hawks are to Southern California what northern goshawks (*A. gentilis*), are to the mountains and coniferous forests of the Pacific Northwest and Alaska, powerful and essential predators keeping other animal populations in check through prodigious hunting.

Although the magnificent peregrine is the largest falcon in North America and occurs as both resident and migrant in our area, we also have much smaller falcons in our midst. The American kestrel (*Falco sparverius*) is a beautiful, dainty, masked falcon, the stunning males draped in a rust-orange and blue-gray mantle and a black mask. Kestrels are most often seen hovering above open fields as they scan the ground beneath for mice, lizards, and other small prey. They're common almost everywhere in the western hemisphere, with related species found across much of Africa and Asia too. The kestrel's somewhat larger cousin, the merlin (*F. columbarius*), is also a falcon of open country, but it prefers to hunt other birds. In some parts of the United States, Merlins are the more commonly seen small falcon, but in Southern California they play second fiddle to the ubiquitous kestrel.

Sometimes the black-winged silhouette that Angelenos spot soaring overhead is a bird that doesn't hunt at all. Turkey vultures (*Cathartes aura*) are among the most common carnivorous birds in

North America. But they don't actually prey on anything except the carcasses of dead animals. The telltale odor of a dead deer in a canyon or a pile of trash in an urban area brings dozens or hundreds of vultures. Their strong sense of smell distinguishes them from most birds; vultures can home in on the scent of rotting meat from miles away. They alight on tree limbs and power lines, often roosting in the area while waiting for a chance to pull some flesh from the carcass. In the morning, they wait for the air to warm up so they can ride the thermal lifts without expending their energy flapping their wings. They glide in great circles, or kettles, their long wings held in a lovely V-shape that identifies them from a great distance.

Both of the two large eagle species that occur in North America—the golden *(Aquila chrysaetos)* and the bald *(Haliaeetus leucocephalus)*— are seen in the vicinity of Los Angeles. Bald eagles nest on the Channel Islands offshore, and soar and swoop around fishing boats in the channel between LA and the islands. Golden eagles rarely cross the Los Angeles basin, but they can be seen an hour's drive away, perched in tall trees or soaring over the higher mountains ringing our area.

When darkness falls across suburban Los Angeles, the hawks, falcons, and vultures settle down to roost for the night, and an entirely different array of birds of prey appear. The rhythmic hoo-ing of great horned owls *(Bubo virginianus)* reverberates throughout the night, not only in our area but nearly across the entire western hemisphere. The great horned owl is a magnificent nocturnal predator, regal and silent yet confiding enough to sit calmly as your flashlight's beam finds it in an oak tree in your yard. The other large owl in our backyards is equally cosmopolitan. The barn owl *(Tyto alba)* doesn't hoot at all, but its piercing shrieks lead unsuspecting residents to wonder what's being drawn and quartered halfway up the tree. Barn owls live and nest in tree cavities and under eaves all around us; a well-placed owl nest box may lure them to raise their owlets right next to your bedroom window, although you'll have to put up with the raucous screams of a nest full of babies for a few months. A barn owl in your yard means an eager devourer of hundreds of rats and mice per year, so we should welcome them. If you find owl pellets on the ground near a tree—the congealed mass of indigested bony bits of the owls' rodent diet—then you're fortunate enough to have owls in your neighborhood.

The third owl that commonly resides in our suburbs is more often heard than seen, and its enigmatic, un-owlish voice confuses many first-time listeners. The rapid, bouncing calls of the western screech owl *(Megascops kennicottii)* very much resemble the sound of a ping-pong ball dropped on a table. Western screeches are beautiful little owls, usually slaty gray in our area. They're hard to see; by standing patiently in your backyard at night, you might end up right under one as it sits in an oak or under a power line staring down at you.

Several other owl species live a stone's throw from the LA basin. The burrowing owl *(Athene cunicularia)* occurs in agricultural areas and deserts outside Los Angeles; it also makes appearances in places like the fields around Los Angeles International Airport. The spotted owl *(Strix occidentalis)* is a largish bird, better known in Northern California as an iconic species of old-growth conifer forests. But it occurs in the Los Angeles basin too; I've seen spotted owls looking down at me in tree-filled canyons in the San Gabriel Mountains, a forty-minute drive from downtown LA. Those same mountains have populations of other rarely seen owl residents, like the long-eared *(Asio otus)*, saw-whet *(Aegolius acadicus)*, and flammulated *(Psiloscops flammeolus)* owls. Seeing these beautiful, secretive species requires a night or two spent searching and listening high in the mountains behind my Pasadena home.

Most raptor populations have declined with increasing urbanization. Nesting trees have disappeared along with a diverse food supply, and the general, noisy chaos of humanity is stressful to them. A few species, like red-tails and Cooper's, have held their own, able to take advantage of human-assisted food in the form of vast supplies of rodents, or birds congregating around backyard feeders. The sheer abundance of a few species belies the overall harm done to raptor biodiversity by our ever-expanding suburbs and subdivisions. Protecting our community of raptors is as essential as anything else we can do to be eco-conscious. Preserving large native trees and green space overall, along with reducing the use of rodenticides, would go a long way toward ensuring our birds of prey have a future in Los Angeles.

18

Not Even the Squirrels Belong

Every spring the squirrels hit my yard like a gang of juvenile delinquent skateboarders discovering a new park in which to have some illegal fun. New litters have grown up and left the nest, and suddenly three or four young squirrels adopt my trees and bushes as their new playground. They are nothing if not entertaining. I know people who befriend their backyard squirrels as quasi-pets, feeding them at the patio table, keeping track of their comings and goings, and generally adoring them.

Like nearly every suburban area in the United States, Los Angeles had a local squirrel. It was the western gray squirrel *(Sciurus griseus)*, a tree-loving, seed-eating squirrel that is the western counterpart to

the eastern gray squirrel *(S. carolinensis)*, a familiar creature of forests, parks, and suburbs from just west of the Mississippi River, north to Canada, and east to Florida and New England. Western grays are a bit more reclusive than their eastern kin and were apparently never as common in our suburbia as eastern grays are in theirs, preferring more densely and extensively forested hilly areas. They're known to be more sensitive to fragmentation of their habitat than other American squirrel species. They are also susceptible to parasitic diseases like mange, which many believe decimated their population in the Los Angeles basin a century ago.

Other squirrels live in our area too. The California ground squirrel *(Otospermophilus beecheyi)* is common in some areas and could be confused with a gray squirrel if you didn't notice the former's stubbier tail. The northern flying squirrel *(Glaucomys sabrinus)* is a dainty species of the San Bernadino Mountains to the east of the basin.

The villain in our squirrel story is the species I described frequenting my yard, an unlikely villain in its charming antics and appearance:

the eastern fox squirrel *(S. niger)*. Visually, it's a beautiful animal, gray fur with frosted tips and a contrasting burnt-orange belly and throat, the color extending into the tail and up onto the face. Ecologically, it's a horror show. The eastern fox squirrel is highly versatile and adapts well to suburban and even urban landscapes. It reproduces rapidly, eats everything in sight, and can be destructive to property.

The origin story of invasive squirrels in Los Angeles sounds a bit like urban legend, but is by all accounts historical fact. In the early 1900s, a veterans hospital on the west side of Los Angeles (at Wilshire and Sepulveda Boulevards) housed and cared for Civil War veterans, some of whom hailed from midwestern states. Now in LA, these veterans longed to see the local squirrels they had grown up with and managed to import some fox squirrels from the East. Inevitably, some eventually escaped and began breeding in the vicinity of the hospital grounds.

If this seems unlikely, it may help to know that until the twentieth century, squirrels were quite popular as pets in the United States. They were sold in pet shops, but more often taken from the wild as babies and raised at home. Dainty flying squirrels were especially popular due to their gentle nature and adorableness, and despite their nocturnal habits. But people also commonly kept tree squirrels like grays and foxes. Benjamin Franklin had a pet squirrel named Mungo, shipped to him as a gift while he lived in England. Mungo was cared for lovingly until he escaped and was killed by a local dog. As recently as seventy-five years ago, a pet squirrel lived in the White House with President Harry Truman. Squirrels generally make awful pets, prone to biting and scratching. But pet squirrels were most definitely a thing a century and more ago. In fact, squirrels first populated city parks across the country when they were intentionally introduced as adorable, decorative creatures to please picnickers.

Other fox squirrel introductions have been made throughout Southern California, even after they were banned decades ago. Today it is against the law to translocate squirrels because so many transfers have gone sideways and resulted in disease transmission or unwanted squirrels in new places. The results of earlier transloca-tions have been great for the fox squirrel diaspora, but very bad for the local native gray squirrels.

Fox squirrels have double the reproductive output of gray squir-rels, producing two litters yearly to the latter's one. It didn't take long for fox squirrels to begin an inexorable spread across the Los Angeles basin, up the coast into Ventura County, and down the coast to Orange County (although they are still compara-tively rare to the south of the Los Angeles area). Since, according to some reconstructions, western gray squirrels had already seen their numbers in the basin plunge due to disease, it wasn't hard for fox squirrels to take over. Within a few decades, fox squirrels had largely vanquished their smaller, less aggressive competitors. The eastern population of gray squirrels evolved in the same place as fox squirrels, no doubt offering them some adaptations that enabled both to coexist. No such benefits helped western grays, which in the absence of a naturally competing species, weren't able to with-stand competition for food or nesting sites or to keep up with the fox squirrels' fecund breeding habits. These days, gray squirrels are rare to nonexistent in our region below about a thousand feet of hilly elevation.

In Los Angeles proper, the best place to see western grays, and also to see both species living in proximity to one another, is Griffith Park. A remarkable four-thousand-acre mixture of forest, parks, riding and hiking trails, and a few tourist attractions like the famed Hollywood Sign, Greek Theater, and Griffith Observatory,

Griffith is one of the largest urban parks in the United States. The western gray squirrels of Griffith Park are a remnant population of their former range in the region. A recent study by Christopher DeMarco and his colleagues confirmed that the Griffith Park gray squirrels show little genetic variation and have a high proportion of related animals, all classic symptoms of isolation due to habitat fragmentation. The study also suggested a high possibility of extirpation in the not-distant future. Although DeMarco and colleagues don't link the presence of eastern fox squirrels to the decline and isolation of western grays, it's certainly one contributing factor to their likely future demise.

The one bailiwick of western gray squirrels, which eastern fox squirrels have yet to penetrate, is the mountains. Fox squirrels have not successfully colonized the foothills that rim Los Angeles north and east, though in a few cases they have managed to strike an uneasy coexistence with western grays. Higher in the mountains, western grays are firmly in their element, and they have the forests all to themselves. The best place I know of to sit and watch western grays going about their business is on the upper slopes of Mount Wilson, in the San Gabriel range behind Pasadena. The stands of pine trees atop Mount Wilson surrounding the famed observatory teem with western grays, happily foraging for pine cones without worrying about their aggressive lowland cousins.

Why does it matter? Some might say that a squirrel is a squirrel. You might even argue for survival of the prettiest—that fox squirrels are more attractive and so more enjoyable to see in your local park, so maybe we should celebrate their ascendancy over grays rather than object to it. The fact is, the Los Angeles basin and its surrounding mountains *belong* to the western gray squirrel. Their history in our area dates back millions of years. Their ecology and the essential role that they play in our ecosystem is linked with that of our local forests, especially seed-producing trees. Just as non-native plants don't sustain native insects, invasive rodents like fox squirrels, with no history in our area, may not do the same job of dispersing seeds that gray squirrels do. Beyond any symbolic historical roots, the replacement of one species over another has implications for the functioning of our local ecosystems.

19

Not Your Average Bear

The social media app in my neighborhood is full of posts intended to enlighten, complain, or just be neighborly. But the most-viewed posts, with accompanying videos, are always those about wildlife. The mountain lion that was spotted lapping water from a neighbor's swimming pool. The peacock that pecked at the paint job on someone's new car. The pack of coyotes that followed a dog walker for blocks. The bear posts stand out in particular. In Los Angeles, if you live near the mountain front, you're eventually going to have a bear encounter, and when you do, you'll have major wildlife encounter cred. It's a story you will tell at parties and little league games for the rest of your natural life, and your video clip posted to Facebook or

Instagram just might go viral and gain you a few thousand followers.

Encounters with mountain lions in Los Angeles are so rare and fleeting that the cats seem almost mythical. Bears, on the other hand, amble into backyards, poke their noses into screen doors, rummage through the trash, and let their cubs take a dip in the family swimming pool. They live in the mountains and canyons rimming Los Angeles, venturing out into the neighborhoods in search of food. Our local population of black bears may number in the hundreds and has been increasing steadily, although is still small compared to the forty thousand-plus black bears estimated statewide. Unlike a big cat's sleek, graceful movements and ominously baleful stare, a black bear seems downright comical as it ambles and gambols and cavorts. Very rare injuries to people usually happen when people fail to treat a bear with the basic level of respect due a large wild animal armed with large teeth and claws.

Bears have a deep history in the Los Angeles basin, as any visitor to the La Brea Tar Pits and Museum can tell you. Thousands of years ago, the giant short-faced bear *(Arctodus simus)* roamed Southern California, and dozens of fossil specimens of this behemoth have been found in the tar deposits. The giant short-faced bear was far larger than any living bear in size and weight, standing more than five feet tall at the shoulder, and reaching more than ten feet tall when standing bipedally. These apex predators were recorded as recently as twelve thousand years ago in our area, and went extinct from unknown causes, perhaps related to the extinction of large hoofed animals that they likely hunted and scavenged.

The bears living in the Los Angeles basin today are black

bears *(Ursus americanus)*, which live throughout North America: the backcountry of Yellowstone, the swamps of the Everglades, and across Canada and Alaska. They're also found in suburban neighborhoods from Anchorage to New York City. While black bears occur naturally throughout the Sierra Nevada in central and Northern California, all our local black bears are reportedly descendants of twenty-seven bears that were relocated from the Yosemite National Park area to the San Gabriel and San Bernadino Mountains in the 1930s. I'm skeptical about this as their sole origin, simply because of the tendency for large highly adaptable mammals to disperse naturally, often following human settlements and their detritus.

With such an enormous range, there are many local variants. Ours is the California black bear *(U. a. californiensis)*. Some populations, including the one that occurs in the Los Angeles basin, include "cinnamon" bears that are tan or brown. They're relatively small in our area; a big adult male weighs in around two hundred pounds and females up to one hundred fifty. In areas with a greater abundance of ideal food, black bears can reach far larger sizes. But they are all puny when compared to the bear with which they once shared habitats across the American West: the grizzly bear *(Ursus arctos horribilis)*.

Grizzlies in North America are a local variant of the gigantic brown bears that live across Canada, much of Alaska, and the northern reaches of Europe. There was a time when grizzlies roamed Southern California, and after the extinction of the giant short-faced bear, they became the region's apex predators. We think of grizzlies as mountain animals, because most of us see them in rugged places like Yellowstone and Glacier National Parks. Historically, however, they once lived in all sorts of ecosystems, including river valleys, plains, and the seacoast. The huge stands of California black oak trees *(Quercus kelloggii)* that cover the foothills of the Sierra

Nevada were feasting grounds for grizzlies as they fattened up on acorns before winter set in.

Early European colonizers of the Los Angeles basin worried about them but also exploited them; bear-baiting was a gruesome form of entertainment in the nineteenth century. And then they were gone. Grizzlies were mostly extirpated from California by the mid-1800s, and entirely by the early twentieth century. The very last grizzly in the state was shot in 1922 in Central California, and the last grizzly in Southern California was killed even earlier, in 1916. Although there were unconfirmed sightings after that, for practical purposes the California grizzly had ceased to exist, though its image still brands everything from beer to the official flag of the state of California.

Historically, grizzlies likely controlled the open country, limiting black bears to forest habitat. Today, black bears range the state in a wide variety of habitats. Unlike grizzlies, which pose a rare but life-threatening risk when we hike in their foraging grounds, black bears are very rarely aggressive to people and generally do their best to get away from us, even when molested or approached too closely. In the past thirty-five years, there have been a total of one hundred attacks by black bears on people in the state of California, only five of which occurred in Southern California. Severe or lethal attacks on humans are a one-in-a-million scenario and often involve dogs; typically, a bear is attacked by a dog or dogs near a home, and the bear fights back. The dog owner tries to intercede to protect his or her pets, or the dog retreats to the owner, and the bear then turns its attention to the human, with tragic consequences. A recent viral video showed a young woman defending her dogs against a large bear perched on her backyard wall. As the bear leaned into her yard, swatting its big paws at the canines, she ran into the yard and forcefully shoved the bear off the wall and out of the yard. Most bear biologists who have spent thousands of hours around black bears regard them as innocuous, eager to avoid confrontation, and backing down from conflict with humans 99.9 percent of the time. Unlike dogs, which can be extremely territorial and prone to bite when their space is intruded upon, black bears typically flee from such encounters. You are certainly far more likely to be attacked by a dog than by a bear in an equal number of close encounters with each.

It's a good thing that black bears pose little danger to people, because they regularly leave their mountain habitat and amble down suburban streets. As I was writing this chapter, a bear was spotted wandering through Eagle Rock, a northern suburb of Los Angeles. Eagle Rock is at its closest point nearly eight miles from any canyon or extension of Angeles National Forest. Assuming the bear made its way into the community on its own, it must have traveled through several towns without being seen.

Most bears are omnivores. Even Alaskan grizzlies that don't live near salmon streams tend to eat a diet of berries, plants, and small animals like squirrels and rodents. Black bears are the ultimate omnivores; they may have the size and agility to bring down a large deer, but their normal diet mainly includes insects, berries, grasses, acorns, and the like. Catching a squirrel or fawn is a rare bounty. Their catholic diet makes them highly adaptable to human habitation. Coming out of their canyons and hills to rummage through garbage cans, pet food dishes, and anything edible left out by people is just being a good opportunistic omnivore.

While bears don't necessarily project an appearance of great intellect, studies of bear cognition have shown that they have relatively high-level skills when it comes to, for instance, number counting. Math cognitive ability is often seen in highly social animals living in long-term, stable groups, who must manage the complexities of remembering their web of relationships with groupmates, allies, and nemeses. Primates, wolves, elephants, dolphins, and whales all show mathematical ability. The adaptive benefit of a bear's ability to distinguish large from small quantities isn't immediately clear, but it's an example of underappreciated intelligence in a mammal that is quite far from our family tree.

Like most mammals, black bears are not particularly social. They congregate only when a food source draws them to the same place. In late spring, after two years growing up under the watchful eye of mom, black bears begin to disperse to find their own foraging grounds. As with nearly all mammals, males tend to disperse farther than females. This is usually because a female must be intimately familiar with her habitat in order to nourish herself and her cubs. A male's essential need consists mostly of finding female bears during mating season. So, as with mountain lions and many other species, it's usually young male bears that come into contact with people as they wander out of the mountains in search of food and a good place to call their foraging grounds.

So-called "problem bears" have learned that humans leave their food and edible trash exposed. Problem bears are, in other words, created by problem humans. Bears are powerful, and breaking into a house, car, or any poorly secured food or trash container is easy work for them. There are only two ways to deal with the problem: remove the desirable food or trash, or remove the bear. All too often it's the bear that is removed. In more rural areas on the edge of the Los Angeles basin, people keep livestock, poultry, and orchards, and bears have been known to prey on all of these.

It's a wonderful thing to have a magnificent big mammal roaming the confines of one of the world's largest and most sprawling metropolises. It's also a responsibility. Our relationship with black bears is vastly different from our relationship with mountain lions. Unlike the big cats, bears are common, encountered by residents regularly, and fed by the refuse of humanity. There is a bear hunting season in California, controversial not only for ethical reasons but also because the status of our bear population is uncertain. The Department of Fish and Wildlife has for years estimated a black bear population of thirty to forty thousand in the state, but recent estimates have lowered this to as few as ten to twenty thousand. Yet the bear hunts continue. There is little reason to think our local Los Angeles bear population is threatened. Instead, the issue may be that as people build homes deeper into our canyons, encounters will increase, sometimes with unfortunate outcomes for which the bears, rather than the people, are too often blamed.

20

Love 'Em
or Hate 'Em

In Los Angeles suburbia, raccoons engender polarizing viewpoints. They're adorable, clever, inquisitive, furry backyard visitors. They're also brazen, obnoxious beasts that will enter your home through the cat door, ransack your trash, attack your dogs, and gobble up your koi, destroying the pond and surrounding garden in the process. As much as I admire raccoon smarts, I fall into the latter camp of residents who just wish the raccoons would stay away, and I've devised various humane ways to try to keep them out of my yard. They're attracted to trash, pet food, fish ponds, fruit trees, bird feeders and . . . just about anything in a suburban yard that could feed an always-ravenous omnivore.

Across Los Angeles and most other places where Americans live, raccoon stories abound. The raccoons who came into a newly sodded yard and rolled up the lawn in search of earthworms and grubs underneath. The raccoons who awakened me at 2:00 a.m. with the sound of crunching: the shells of the turtles that lived in my backyard pond. (My bad for not having electric fencing or a net for protection.) I have a friend whose large tortoise was decapitated and de-limbed by a hungry—or perhaps just sadistic—raccoon. Accounts of pets being attacked by a raccoon, or even by a pack of them, are increasingly common. Residents are divided into the "get rid of them by whatever means necessary" camp, and the "we need to show respect for their lives in order to respect all life" camp. Many people live-trap nuisance raccoons and release them miles away. As with squirrels, such translocating is technically illegal—due to concerns over disease transmission if the animal is unhealthy—but rarely enforced. Raccoons, like other wildlife, are also protected by law against inhumane killing, although the definition of inhumane is a bit vague. A raccoon dropped in unfamiliar territory, inside the home range of other raccoons, probably has a lower chance of survival than it did on its lifelong stomping grounds, but the trapper normally doesn't factor this into the decision to remove it.

As with squirrels, in times past raccoons represented something very different to Americans. As fur bearers, they were valued for their warm, beautiful pelts; Native American peoples, and later, European colonists, valued coonskin as a garment material. Coonskin hats with raccoon tails feature prominently in American folk history; the Davy Crockett hats in the television shows of the mid-twentieth century fueled a harvest of millions of raccoons annually.

Raccoons were once also valued as food. I spent my summers in college working in a steel foundry in New Jersey, helping the men who poured molten steel. The work crews were mostly men who had moved north from the Deep South in search of work, some from rural towns, and the elders among them discussed recipes they recalled for both racoon and opossum meat. Cookbooks as recently as the 1940s contained recipes for raccoon meat, right alongside recipes for preparing venison and duck.

Like squirrels, raccoons were also once valued as pets, though their tendency to bite makes them—especially adult males—less than ideal pets. Yet, President Calvin Coolidge had a pet raccoon in the White House.

Raccoons were naively introduced to Europe from North America in the last century and now occur across most of that continent. I have friends in Germany—which has the largest raccoon population outside the United States—and Austria who cringe at the mention of the animals because of the damage they have done to pets and property since being introduced to Europe and spreading far and wide.

The children's book *Rascal,* written by Sterling North about a pet raccoon, led to a movie and then an animated television series. The show was a hit in Japan, leading to the importation of thousands of raccoons for the pet trade. Some were inevitably released, and they have spread everywhere and now wreak havoc on property and native Japanese animals. Historical and archaeological evidence suggest that while raccoons are native to California, their densities were dramatically lower in the past than today, and their numbers have followed human settlement patterns in the nineteenth and twentieth centuries here as well as across North America.

Raccoons are marauders par excellence, and not only in their native range. Although their native habitat is woodlands and swamplands, they love agricultural areas and the crops they provide—their damage to cornfields is legendary—and they love suburbia; these days, raccoons are certainly more abundant in urban and suburban areas than in forests. In the Los Angeles basin, they've been accused of tearing off roofing and shingling material, ventilation ducts, and insulation to enter attics to make nests. They're well-known residents under houses, porches, and garages. Once ensconced in a house or attic, their urine and feces, as well as the parasites they often harbor, become a homeowner's nightmare.

Raccoon feces carry a roundworm specific to raccoons (roundworm eggs are present in the droppings of practically every animal that enters your yard), which can infect and sicken pets and, in rare cases, people. Raccoons are the second most common animal vector of rabies in the United States (after bats), with nearly a third of all recorded cases in the past fifty years, albeit mainly in the eastern US, not in California. They tend to succumb to the virus very rapidly if infected and don't pose a measurable threat to human health.

But there's also much to appreciate about raccoons. Comparative psychologists often use them as subjects in studies of animal intelligence, which show them to be impressively smart, outperforming dogs on tests intended to measure animal cognition. Researchers regard them as one of the most highly intelligent non-primates in the animal world. Their intense curiosity about objects, combined with their highly dexterous paws, contribute to their cognitive prowess. When captive raccoons are presented with a puzzle box that they need to open to reach a reward, they problem-solve in innovative ways, finding multiple solutions to the same puzzle. Their intelligence may contribute to their incredible adaptability as well as their ubiquity as an invasive species on three continents.

Smarts aside, raccoons are attractive animals, with lush fur coats (at least in our area; in warmer climes they tend to be shorter haired with a far scrawnier look), and a certain charm. In early spring you may hear males fighting loudly during mating season. Females birth in spring and summer to litters of several kits. A mama raccoon ambling across a lawn with several babies in tow attracts an admiring crowd of onlookers who gush about her maternal instincts.

In a natural ecosystem, raccoons have a part to play, just like every other animal species. They are prey for coyotes, bobcats, and mountain lions. They eat a considerable quantity of fruits, the seeds of which they excrete and thereby disperse, aiding the reproductive efforts of many trees. Their love of human trash is testimony to their natural role as ecosystem scavengers, eating carrion and removing diseased carcasses from the landscape. And they are important predators on parasitic species like wasps. Raccoons also eat any small animal they can catch, reducing burgeoning rat and mouse populations in suburbia. The downside of their omnivorousness is that they also catch and eat native birds in their nests. And attractive nuisances like open trash containers, fish ponds, pet food, or newly laid sod will always attract them.

Far more people in Southern California live in close contact with raccoons than with bears, mountain lions, or bobcats. And given how abundant and destructive the masked marauders can be, avoidance and management of racoons may be more important than avoidance and management of these other species we tend to fear more. Raccoons are said to avoid bright lights, such as motion-sensitive outdoor lights; I know people who swear by small flashing strobe lights—just a tiny point of blinking red light—to keep them out of a backyard at night. Others swear that lights don't deter them for long.

Motion-activated sprinklers are supposed to repel racoons with water. But with other animals passing through, those sprinklers may end up being on a lot. It can help to clear hedges and overhanging trees from the property line to give a raccoon fewer points of easy entry to a yard. Raccoons allegedly hate the odors of ammonia, dog or coyote urine, cucumber plants, peppermint oil, Epsom salts, garlic, cayenne pepper, and the scent of a rival boar (male) raccoon. I've never tested any of those myself, and you will find doubters who have tried everything and still have raccoons living under their garage or in their attic.

Although racoons sometimes fight with dogs, the presence of a dog or even its odor is likely to deter raccoons too. If all else fails, live-trapping an offending raccoon and translocating it to an appropriate habitat many miles away is, though technically illegal, effective. Because of their aforementioned intelligence, raccoons can be trap savvy if they've been caught before. And it's worth pointing out that as with many animal species, dropping them into a completely unknown location, probably within the home range of other established raccoons, is likely to lead to aggressive encounters with the resident raccoon population.

The irony of our raccoon predicament is that we've encouraged and even trained them to colonize our landscape. We surround ourselves with trash and discarded food, pet food on porches, and warm places to sleep in our attics and garages. The barriers and deterrents that we erect in a largely futile attempt to keep raccoons at bay has often led them to their advanced problem-solving. Some researchers have suggested that, as a result, urban raccoons possess cognitive skills that rural raccoons lack. There is no reason to think that the raccoon population will do anything but grow in coming decades; only a disease outbreak is likely to stem it, and that would be a temporary setback. The hordes of raccoons that are an integral part of our suburban lives are here to stay, love 'em or hate 'em.

21

Dumpster Divers and Backyard Stinkers

Like so many suburbanites, my first look at an opossum was spying the long, gnarly, naked tail of the biggest, shaggiest rat I'd ever seen, hunched over my cat's outdoor food dish. When he didn't respond to my yell, I should have clued into the fact that this was no mere rat. With much coaxing he finally ambled off, and I haven't made the mistake of feeding (or keeping) a cat outdoors in the many years since.

Opossums are native to the eastern United States and now live across most of North America. Our local Virginia opossums (*Didelphis virginiana*) were introduced to Southern California in the late 1800s, possibly as a food source for immigrants from the southeastern states, for whom opossum was a delicacy. Opossum pelts were also valued for their fur, as unlikely as that may seem today.

Our local opossum is the size of a house cat, with males larger than females. That rat-like naked tail that repulses many people is somewhat prehensile, and helps the opossum grip branches as it climbs. Despite this adaptation, opossums spend most of their lives on the ground, sleeping the days away under brush piles, garages, houses, and porches, coming out at night to forage in the neighborhood. Opossums mark their foraging areas with their urine, feces, and a scent that comes from a gland in their neck, creating a signpost of activity that wards off other opossums.

Their famed habit of playing dead is an effective anti-predator tactic: by lying inert for many minutes—or even hours—they avoid triggering a predatory response in the animal posing a threat. Opossums stop playing dead in captivity when acclimated to human contact. When I've picked up young opossums wandering around my backyard, they tend to flash a toothy wide-open mouth for a few seconds, then drop all pretense of aggression and calmy sit in my hand.

I have colleagues and friends who have raised orphaned opossums and found them to be sweet-natured creatures, despite their tendency to hiss, growl, or expose their teeth when frightened. Despite all appearances, opossums are neither vicious nor unintelligent.

The Virginia opossum's incredibly catholic diet has enabled its success as a species. Opossums eat nearly anything found in a suburban backyard, from earthworms and slugs to fruit to bird eggs to household garbage and pet food. In that sense they perform an underappreciated role as scavengers, ridding our suburban ecosystem of carrion and other detritus. A backyard also provides an ideal place to find shelter in or under garages, decks, trash heaps, and wood piles. Unlike raccoons, opossums are not brazen predators.

That koi who goes missing from your pond was almost certainly not taken by an opossum, nor does the opossum pose a threat to your cat or your child.

Opossums can be purveyors of diseases like leptospirosis, either through their urine or feces, or through their saliva; an infected opossum could nibble a fallen piece of fruit, which you then unwisely take a bite from. The parasites that travel along with opossums—ticks and fleas and such—carry diseases too. On the other hand, opossums seem to have resistance to many viral diseases that racoons and other suburban mammals carry, like rabies, distemper, and parvovirus, carrying little risk of infecting dogs or people.

Opossums offer tantalizing clues for improving human health. Their spinal cords can regenerate from severe damage in the days following birth. They have also demonstrated immunity to the bites of venomous snakes; their blood contains a protein, Lethal Toxin-Neutralizing Factor (LTNF), that protects them against rattlesnake and other viper bites.

The clattering sounded clearly like claws on a hardwood floor, coming from my dining room. As I got up from the sofa and walked to the next room to see what the commotion was about, it occurred to me that my cat, with his retractable claws, would not make a sound like that. And I did not have a dog. In the dining room, I saw my cat under the table, cavorting playfully with a skunk. The skunk was half grown, certainly not an adult, and since the front door was standing open, it was obvious he had waddled in from his evening rounds of the neighborhood and was now having a good time with my cat. It is a challenge to get a skunk out of your house while avoiding a spray. I closed all the other doors, and used a broom to very gently suggest that he should find another playmate. It worked. The cat lost a new friend, but I saved my family from the stench.

Ask anyone to describe a skunk and you will always get the same response: a mention of their noxious spray. We're all familiar with the odor wafting into our cars as we drive, telling us a skunk didn't make it across the roadway. From a distance, I find the odor vaguely pleasant; but being sprayed at close range can have a burning, stomach-turning effect. The spray comes from two tiny sacs and is an alkaline sulphurous concoction of organic compounds that are also found in onions and garlic. Getting a full dose in the face is like getting a dose of tear gas.

Removing the odor is anything but easy. Supposedly a grease-cutting dish detergent and baking soda bath can work for both body and clothing. The time-honored tomato juice remedy may temporarily mask the odor, but will not make it disappear. If you've been sprayed, your nose will be so overwhelmed with skunk odor that the tomato juice can seem to work. To those less inured to the smell, the odor will be as intensely awful as ever.

Skunks and their ancestors have been around for tens of millions of years, evolving from the same ancestral carnivores as weasels and European polecats. Unlike opossums and some of the other small mammals that live here, our skunks are natives to Southern California, as well as to much of the United States. We have two species in the Los Angeles basin, although we humans only encounter one of them frequently: the housecat-sized striped skunk *(Mephitis mephitis)*. I have never seen a spotted skunk *(Spilogale gracilis)* in our area, although this much daintier animal does occur here and is common in much of the United States and Mexico. The spotted skunk has been the subject of much recent genetic research showing that climate change over the past million years split their ancestors' habitat, and subsequently their DNA, into several population clusters, which are visually almost identical but substantially different at the genetic level.

The word *skunk* comes from an Algonquian word for the animal, and the name of the city of Chicago may have been derived from an Ojibwe word for it. The Ojibwe and Menominee creation stories feature giant skunks, or people transformed into skunks. Locally, the Tongva make mention of the *poniivo* (skunk) in their lore as well.

Skunks are well adapted to the life of a grub-digging, ground-dwelling scavenger, armed with claws that can tear apart rotting wood in search of such food. They also hunt frogs and fish in our local canyons. Skunks' vivid black-and-white aposematic—warning—pattern is its calling card, warding off would-be predators long before they approach close enough to warrant an olfactory assault. Few natural predators are daring enough to hunt them; mountain lions, bobcats, coyotes, foxes, badgers, and owls are all known to eat skunks, but apparently on rare occasions only.

Usually solitary and nocturnal, skunks become social in two seasons. In winter they sometimes den communally underground or under a Los Angeles garage or porch, and in early spring they become more active during the mating season. Reaching sexual maturity in their first year, males roam far and wide in search of females, entering backyards and into contact with other males. Meanwhile, females begin searching for future denning sites under houses and decks. Females also spray more often to deter the affections of some males, and this is when most human encounters with skunks occur. Like opossums, female skunks can pause the embryonic development of their offspring for up to a few weeks, presumably if conditions of food and nutrition warrant more time. After a two-month gestation, females give birth to several kits. They're weaned within two months;

females sometimes mate and reproduce a second time in late spring. Their lifespan in the wild is just a few years.

As with other small North American mammals, there is a long history of people keeping skunks as household pets. In decades past they were considered reasonably well-behaved captives, as long as their scent glands were removed. Modern ethics about animals regard removing the scent glands as abusive, not unlike declawing a house cat and leaving it defenseless if it escapes outdoors. Growing up in suburban New Jersey, I knew a family with a pet skunk. She was mostly nocturnal, wandering the house at night. She was housebroken to use a litter box, with some success, and she was also prone to bite people who handled her roughly. Generations of striped skunks have been bred for their pelts and, to a far lesser extent, for the pet trade, although state laws restricting the keeping and selling of native wild animal species—originally to prevent the spread of rabies— have largely and wisely eliminated this practice.

Like opossums and many other local mammals, skunks can carry diseases. They carry rabies less frequently than raccoons, but still represent nearly a quarter of all rabid bites in the United States in some years. Still, there has been only one confirmed case of skunk-to-human transmission in Los Angeles in the past forty years. For the most part, skunks are beneficial to our landscape. Like their fellow-omnivore opossums, skunks eat trash, pet food, and the general detritus of the suburbs. By closing off the openings under our houses, garages, and decks, and keeping pet food indoors and trash securely covered, we can begin to regard these animals—whose tails are often the last thing we'd want to see—as suburban allies. They enrich our lives and ask only to be given some space to lead their own. To be honest, I would miss the pungent odor of skunk spray if I didn't smell it once in a while.

V.

REMARKABLE NEIGHBORS

22

The Smart Ones

The large black bird struts over to a beaker of water. The water is shallow, and a fat floating worm is wriggling in it. The bird cocks his head as if trying to understand the problem here—no way to reach the tasty worm given the low level of the water in the container. A moment's pause, and then the bird—a rook, a European relative of the American crow—steps over to a pile of stones of various sizes conveniently left at the spot. He picks the stones up one by one and drops them into the beaker. The water level rises with the addition of each stone, until the worm is within reach. He plucks his treat from the rising water and gulps it down.

If this scenario sounds familiar, it's because it was one of Aesop's Fables, "The Crow and the Pitcher," written down some 2,500 years ago after an even more ancient oral history as a moral tale. More recently, researchers in the United Kingdom set out to investigate whether corvids—crows, ravens, magpies, and jays, of which Los Angeles has several species—have the ability to judge the relationship between volume of a liquid and its displacement by a solid. They got more than they bargained for. The rooks learned quickly to use stones instead of other buoyant objects in order to displace the water upward. They selected larger instead of smaller stones to displace more water. Corvid tool use has been well documented for decades. New Caledonian crows, for example, make and use tools in ways that researchers previously thought only humans and chimpanzees could. They pluck twigs from trees and fashion them into hooks, which they use to pry grubs from trees. They also craft certain leaves into probing tools to extract insects and small animals from beneath the soil.

If intelligence is about problem solving, spatial memory, and tool use, then corvids are clearly among the smartest animals on the planet. Corvids have large brains relative to their body size, and they use their brains in obvious ways. Jays and their kin bury nuts and seeds and return to dig them up months later, displaying a spatial memory and reasoning far beyond what we would expect of a bird. Caching one's food requires the jay to understand not only the cache site, but also the perishability of the food and the chances of being watched by would-be food thieves. They return to perishable foods sooner than foods that will keep for a long time without rotting.

Intelligence can also be social; animals that live in large, complex social groups, like humans and many other primates, value social smarts—even social manipulation. In this, some corvids excel too. Bernd Heinrich's wonderful observations of wild ravens in the forest of Maine enlightened us about the intelligence of these large birds. Not only do ravens quickly solve cognitive problems that befuddle crows; they also show complexity in their social interactions that we don't observe in other birds. They are keen students of their own societies, which enables them to manipulate others in their flock. A group of ravens congregating at a roosting tree or an animal carcass are rarely a random, anonymous aggregation. They form long-term, stable bonds that are not simply about breeding, and share food with their closest "friends." Their bonds and share-and-share-alike behaviors give them all more access to food. Ravens recognize the same individuals year after year, and can identify one another by their calls. In all these ways, they resemble primates more than other birds.

In the Los Angeles area, common ravens (*Corvus corax*) are sometimes mistaken for the more abundant American crows (*Corvus brachyrhynchos*), but the species are easily distinguished. At close range, ravens' large size and massive Romanesque bills set them apart, along with their much deeper croaking calls, in contrast to crows' calls of a higher pitch. Seen overhead, a raven's tail has a distinctive diamond shape, in contrast to a crow's squared-off tail. Ravens are the large black birds you commonly see soaring over our local mountains, deserts, and canyons—but also sometimes right over downtown Los Angeles. A pair of ravens, possibly the same pair, nested in a tall pine tree in my neighbor's yard for years. Ravens communicate with a wide variety of calls and sounds, some of which are complex and still not fully understood. From my home office I'd hear the pair chortling, squeaking, and squawking to each other, joined by the calls of their babies in spring. Having these large, impressive birds in our backyard was really a gift.

Crows, formerly birds of forests and farmlands, today inhabit urban and suburban Los Angeles neighborhoods in large numbers. Suburbia is a perfect habitat for crows, with more tall trees for nesting than farmlands, and no angry farmers shooting at them. The suburbs also offer an endless supply of food. I've seen fifty crows gather in the Pasadena area for no apparent reason. Crows mainly flock in the no-breeding winter months, since breeding pairs in spring and summer are not as social. Maybe one crow found an amazing bounty, a trash heap or dead animal, and its calls drew in a few other crows, and their calls drew in more, and so on. Or perhaps there's some larger-order flock coordination going on that we don't fully understand. Dissuading crows from establishing a gathering or nighttime roosting site isn't easy, although loud noises and owl decoys sometimes work.

As residents of our suburbs, crows are still mainly seen as pests. They eat pretty much anything they can get their bills on, including mice, insects, fruit, garbage, and the eggs and young of other birds. Many of the insects they eat are invasive pests, although due to their abundance crows probably decimate some of our native insects, including larvae. The same is true when considering the bird eggs and hatchlings they prey upon.

Ravens and crows have benefited tremendously from the spread of human development, especially from our detritus. Crows normally forage far and wide, fanning out across the Los Angeles area in search of food and flying miles to and from their nighttime roosts. Garbage dumps and landfills are often covered with crows, and these are usually within a few miles of suburbia. Raven populations in the desert areas surrounding Los Angeles have boomed for the same reason, with awful ecological consequences. They are subsidized predators; their subsidy is our trash, which allows their populations to boom and decimate other wild species.

Unfortunately, ravens in the desert towns outside the Los Angeles basin have a taste for our native, threatened desert tortoise. Biologists epoxied radio-transmitters to tortoises' shells and tracked them to nests atop telephone poles and electrical towers. Ravens hunt baby tortoises whose shells are thin enough to be hammered open by a beak, swooping down on hatchlings and spiriting them away to their nests. As raven populations in the desert have boomed, tortoise numbers have plummeted. Conservationists have tried everything from shooting ravens to poisoning them, but have failed due to outcry from animal welfare advocates and the cunning cognition of birds that quickly learn to avoid human attacks. Innovative conservation techniques have included 3-D printed replicas of baby tortoises packed with irritants intended to teach ravens that tortoises are not tasty, and using drones to spray oil onto raven eggs to suffocate the offspring, preventing a new generation of ravens from gobbling up this endangered species. But the sheer abundance of ravens has so far overwhelmed all possible solutions.

One morning while walking up my street in South Pasadena I saw a dead crow in the street. Then another, and another. Over the next two weeks, I saw at least six dead crows in my neighborhood. These were likely victims of West Nile virus, a mosquito-borne disease with a 10 percent mortality rate, which was at the time new in the Los Angeles basin, having arrived in our area in the early 2000s. A second more recent outbreak was also documented, again starting with an infected crow in South Pasadena. While there are no records of bird-to-human transmission, West Nile virus has hit corvid populations, including crows, very hard. Crows are frequent victims because they prey on the eggs, young, and dead bodies of other birds. The mortality rate is nearly 100 percent in crows, and death usually happens within a few days. Like Covid-19, West Nile has mutated time and again; some recent variants are less virulent than those that caused the early slaughter of corvids. Crow populations have largely recovered from this die-off, although conservationists still worry about other corvid species that were less common to begin with.

Although ravens and crows are the largest and most visible corvids in our area, jays are also our corvid neighbors. The western scrub jay (*Aphelocoma californica*), is often misnamed the "blue jay" by Angelenos, confusing the bird with the actual blue jay (*Cyanocitta cristata*) of the eastern United States. Our scrub jay is a beautiful corvid that lives from suburbia all the way to the mountain slopes. In my yard, it's the loud bird with the big bill and long, blue tail that dominates the bird feeders whenever sunflower seeds are offered.

Scrub jays are found all over California. A grayer, less colorful jay occurs farther east in our state. Step off a boat on Santa Cruz Island, part of the Channel Island chain, and it won't take long to spot an island scrub jay (*A. insularis*), an offshoot of the mainland species which, in glorious isolation, has evolved to a visibly larger and more robust size. Another relative outside California, the Florida scrub jay, is famed among bird biologists for its cooperative breeding habits, in which some members of the population operate as helpers to assist parent birds in raising their young.

Other beautiful corvids live not far outside the Los Angeles basin. The Steller's jay (*Cyanocitta stelleri*) is a blue-and-brown crested jay of the higher reaches of our local mountains. The stunning, large black-billed magpie (*Pica hudsonia*) resides in the valleys and mountains north of Los Angeles, and the yellow-billed magpie (*P. nuttalli*) is found only in California just north of our area. These species play a valuable role in local ecosystems as seed cachers and dispersers, depositing acorns and other tree seeds in the ground. They return to their stored bounty later, but some seeds are forgotten and help to repopulate woodlands.

Corvids, with their striking good looks, obvious intelligence, and raucous presence, are among the most iconic of birds, and among the few bird species that may have benefited from expanding human populations. Their conflicts with humanity, old and new, continue to play out in the Southern California landscape.

23

Sage Advice

My first hike in the hills behind Pasadena many years ago was with new friends who had been raised in Southern California. I stopped all along the trail to point excitedly to blossoms, flower stalks, and impressive plants that I had read about but never seen. A massive, sprawling white sage *(Salvia apiana)*, draped itself against a steep hillside. Drifts of California buckwheat *(Eriogonum fasciculatum)* lined the trail, their puffy white flower stalks wobbling in the breeze. When I asked my companions what these were and commented on their delicate beauty, the answers I got back were "some local weed probably," and "I have this stuff in my yard. I mainly do foxgloves and cymbidiums."

Sometimes it takes an outsider with a fresh eye to get excited about native Southern California plants. A lot of out-of-towners have made Los Angeles home, transplanting themselves from the Midwest or back East or another continent altogether. Native California plants may seem exotic and worth cultivating, but the majority of immigrants to the state bring their gardening preferences with them, hence those lush green lawns drowning out the majestic native oaks, and those beds of thirsty tulips and roses soaking up massive quantities of sprinkler water.

The months that most Southern Californians long for—the hot, dry beach weather from July through September—are anathema to our flora. They spend summers just trying to survive the arid heat without dying of desiccation. Winter is when native plants flourish, a time when in most climates the trees and plants are just trying to survive until spring.

In a native plant garden, many local species show their true beauty only in their second or third year after planting. In their first year or two, native plants are more needy of water—sometimes as needy as the nonnatives they've replaced. But by year three if not sooner, natives put on a dramatic seasonal show that rivals that of any flowering plant, without needing regular watering. Native plants also rarely need pesticides, adapted to cope with native wildlife.

For millennia, Indigenous people in the Los Angeles basin have harvested myriad native plants. But it took generations of European Americans to realize that it is more appropriate and environmentally ethical to plant natives in their gardens. The exotic tree planting craze of the late 1800s and early 1900s featured flowering jacarandas (from Brazil; *Jacaranda mimosifolia*), magnolias (usually *Magnolia grandiflora*, from the southeastern United States), and a variety of introduced pines, palms, and maples. Meanwhile, Europeans prized

California natives as exotics; Monterey cypress *(Cupressus macro-carpa)* and California redwoods *(Sequoia sempervirens)* were culti-vated in the United Kingdom and Ireland.

Theodore Payne, a British gardener and landscape designer who immigrated to Southern California as a young man in 1893, is widely regarded as a visionary about the use of California native plants in landscaping. Payne found work as the head gardener for an Orange County estate and developed a lifelong passion for native plants, becoming the doyen of the native plant movement in Los Angeles, recognizing the threats posed by suburban development. He had a hand in designing and planting several of our iconic public gardens, from Descanso Gardens in La Cañada, to Rancho Santa Ana (now known as California Botanic Garden) in Orange County, to Exposi-tion Park in downtown Los Angeles. Most of these spots were orig-inally live oak *(Quercus agrifolia)* woodlands that had been felled. Today, one of the best places to see, learn about, and purchase native plants is the eponymous Theodore Payne Foundation for Wild Flow-ers and Plants in Sun Valley.

Starting in the 1970s and growing steadily into the current cen-tury, a growing water conservation ethic by local and state govern-ments, based on water restrictions and incentivizing lawn removal, brought drought-tolerant plants to the fore. Finally, more Los Ange-les area residents began planting native plants, and a new landscaping style took hold. The neighborhoods at the base of the foothills of the San Gabriel Mountains today feature several houses per block that have either xeriscapes or at least drought-tolerant gardens instead of beds of roses or camelias.

Even as a conservationist, I don't believe in taking an obsessive approach to planting natives in our human-shaped habitat; plenty of nonnative plants are drought tolerant and beautiful. Some of these feed hummingbirds, butterflies and their larvae, bees, and other pollinators. Lavenders *(Lavandula spp.)*, for example, are drought tolerant, beautiful, and covered with bees during spring and summer. Pride of Madeira *(Echium)* send up giant candelabras of purple flowers. But only native plants will provide food throughout the life cycles of many insect species, whose larvae need the species of plant they're adapted to, even if as adults they're flexible about where they harvest their pollen and nectar. One's decision to plant natives, non-natives, or a mix of the two is personal. My current property is about a fifty-fifty mix; in certain shaded spots, a drought-hardy nonnative plant will grow faster and look better than most native choices.

Although there many iconic native flowering plants, the buckwheat (family Polygonaceae) is perhaps the most iconic, and also the most diverse, with more than one hundred species in our state. The California buckwheat *(Eriogonum fasciculatum)* erupts into pinkish-white flower clusters across hillsides and along freeways through our region. It's underappreciated because it's as common as a weed in many areas. But its beauty and hardiness are perfect for a drought garden. The diminutive red buckwheat *(E. grande var. rubescens)* lives in large drifts on the northernmost Channel Islands. At the other extreme, the magnificent Saint Catherine's lace *(E. giganteum)* is a sprawling buckwheat of the more southerly Channel Islands, including the eponymous Catalina Island. Its gnarly branches and gray-green leaves can spread three yards in all directions, and will send up grand flower shoots in spring.

Similarly, the diversity and beauty of our native California sages (genus *Salvia*) never cease to amaze and inspire me. The hills behind LA are covered with white sage *(Salvia apiana)*, which have lovely silvery-green foliage all year and sprout tall flower stalks covered in white in late spring. Among the more colorful sages, nearly all are showy while a few are truly stunning. Black sage *(S. mellifera)* is a sprawling sage, often wider than it is tall, with subtly bluish flowers beloved by pollinators. Cleveland sage *(S. clevelandii)* is found up and down California in nearly every possible habitat and explodes into pale blue flowers in spring. The sages seen in most Los Angeles gardens are hybrids of Cleveland sage with other varieties, creating a crazy quilt mix of profuse colors, and the dainty hummingbird sage *(S. spathacea)*, which pops red flower stalks into the dappled shade of many canyons, fields, and backyard gardens.

Another large group of California natives that are breathtaking in a garden are the so-called California lilacs, the *Ceanothus* (actually in the buckthorn family, Rhamnaceae). This diverse group of dozens of species ranges from ground-hugging, spreading forms—mostly from Northern or Central California but cultivated widely to make hardier varieties for our drier climes—to cultivars that grow upward into trees if given the opportunity. Many native plants grow slowly, but *Ceanothuses* take off quickly; larger species don't stop until they've topped a roof or reached up to the light in a canyon. Their flower clusters range from powder blue to intense purple, and when in bloom, one large plant can be the highlight of a backyard.

While less showy than a *Ceanothus*, the manzanita is one of Southern California's best known plants. There are spreading ground-cover varieties and big bushy varieties; early Spanish settlers called them "little apples" because of their sweet, red clusters of hanging berries. But the bark is their most stunning characteristic; Southern California hikers admire their smooth, brick-red limbs reaching out over trails and into ravines. They're slow growing, tough, and adapted to arid and cold conditions; one of my favorite visions of winter in the San Gabriel Mountains is a flash of manzanita bark peeking out from a snow-covered bush along a trail. Their little flowers also appear in winter. Our most common local species is a huge one, the bigberry manzanita *(Arctostaphylos glauca)*, whose common name reflects the large edible berries it bears in summer. Indigenous peoples have used all parts of the manzanita plant as food and medicine. As a garden plant, manzanitas aren't fond of typical heavily watered suburban conditions, but some varieties adapt to them more easily. Their attractive bark and flowers make them a beautiful, albeit slow-growing, garden addition.

Unlike nearly all other flowering perennials, most monkeyflowers are moisture-loving plants, with tender leaves and eye-popping, colorful flowers. Scarlet monkeyflower *(Erythranthe cardinalis)* is the most familiar of these in our gardens. With adequate water, it's a beautiful perennial, growing naturally in Southern California and Baja California in seepages and wetlands. Cultivars abound, to the extent that it's hard to find the original wild version of the plant in cultivation. In our area, the monkeyflower one finds growing in arid areas is the bush monkeyflower *(Diplacus aurantiacus)*, which bursts forth in huge drifts of golden flowers, carpeting hillsides each spring.

Myriad other native flowering plants deserve our attention. California snapdragons *(Gambelia spp.)* dot hillsides and canyons from the LA basin to the offshore Channel Islands. The island snapdragon *(Gambelia speciosa)* is endangered in the wild, but commonly cultivated in gardens, a showy and easy plant to care for. After seeing its full-bloom spherical starburst of crimson, anyone would choose it over a nonnative flowering plant.

Nonnative mallows *(Lavandula spp.)* are planted frequently in our area, but native mallows *(Malacothamnus spp.)* are equally pretty and also grow quite large. Currants and gooseberries *(Ribes spp.)* put out tasseled, colorful flowers that last for months, although the plants dry up and die off in the late summer heat. Perhaps my favorite larger native flowering plant is the California bush poppy (*Dendromecon harfordii* from the Channel Islands, and *D. rigida* from the mainland). A large bush bordering on small, densely leafed tree, the bush poppy showcases large, yellow flowers in spring.

Finally, a multitude of native plants fit well within, or at the borders of, a traditional lawn space. I've already described some native grasses that are better choices than traditional thirsty turfs. But many flowering plants can also serve as lawns. My favorite is the common yarrow (*Achillea millefolium*), a beautifully lacy plant that grows about a foot tall and has delicate, spreading white flowers. It might be a bit too delicate for a lawn trampled by children every day, but in the right setting, with some light shade, it's stunning. A cultivated hybrid yarrow is hardier than the native species, usually labeled commercially as moonshine yarrow: equally beautiful with yellow instead of white flowers.

Some of the native plants we looked at earlier are also excellent lawn substitutes. Some manzanitas grow as spreading ground covers, as do some *Ceanothuses*. Neither is very pedestrian friendly, but in areas that aren't heavily trodden these plants will look beautiful, and will flower in some seasons too. Coyote brush (*Baccharis pilularis*) is my favored flowering ground cover to replace a thirsty lawn; one cultivar, "pigeon point," is attractive, tough, and extremely drought tolerant, especially on dry slopes.

Succulents have been used for decades in Southern California to landscape everything from yards to industrial parks, from beach access points to outdoor sports stadiums. Nonnative ice plants (*Delosperma spp.*) and chalksticks (*Senecio spp.*) are familiar to anyone in our area. In fact, these have been overplanted due to a mistaken belief that they will do a better job than native plants of holding back soil and preventing sand erosion on hillsides. Enlightened communities are now replacing their ice plants with native buckwheats, *Dudleya*, coyote brush, and others.

The native plants in this chapter provide critical food for native insects, which in turn feed myriad native birds and other wildlife. Planting them restores the key interactions that are the engine of a healthy native ecosystem. As Angelenos move toward a more eco-savvy landscaping ethic, the stunning diversity of our local native plants, formerly limited to canyons and hillsides, needs to be at the forefront of our plans.

24

Lounge Lizards

As I slip into a ragged pair of old running shoes that I use for gardening, my toes hit something soft and squirmy. I extract a flustered male western fence lizard *(Sceloporus occidentalis)*. Cradled in my hand, he shows an impossibly iridescent purple-blue throat and side bands on his belly. In an hour, when the sun toasts the yard, he'll be atop one of the boulders doing territorial push-up displays, his front legs pumping his five-inch body up and down, his blueness puffed out to all the other fence lizards nearby. On a warm, sunny day, a dozen of these little dragons may be lounging in my yard at any given moment. Their social lives are lived in plain view of suburbanites, who too rarely take the time to observe them and appreciate their wildness right in our midst.

Lizards are amazing to me. So many of our local Southern California wildlife are secretive. Even when we encounter them, we usually can't get a sense of their social lives. Although my neighborhood teems with birds, I have no idea where most of them nest and raise their young, or where the migratory species head off to in winter. Coyotes show up mainly at night, and retreat to their private lives in the local canyon by day. But fence lizards are little insect-eating machines that put on a show for us right under our noses. Even warm days in winter bring out a few lizards, cavorting and showing off their territorial conquests. Lizards are incredibly abundant in the LA basin; my suburban neighborhood at the edge of a canyon supports a lizard density far higher than the fifteen to twenty lizards per acre estimated in wild habitats. Lizards rarely stray from the tiny bits of ground where they were hatched; females may occupy only a few thousand square feet (about half an average suburban house plot) their entire lives.

Most of us know precious little about the lizards around our feet. People know that some species can regenerate their tails, a well-placed evolutionary trick when a hungry predator grabs you on your most easily grabbed part. Not all species can regenerate, but many in our area can. It's an ancient and remarkable adaptation: a cartilaginous sheath grows in place of the former tail, encasing a newly regrown spinal cord. Unlike salamanders, which regrow lost limbs and perfect new tails, lizards can't regrow arms or legs, only tails. The severed former tail continues to wriggle furiously for a while, which repulses some people but distracts the would-be predator from the escaping head and body—and that's what matters. The new tail is never quite as good as the original, and studies have shown that the lizard's immune system doesn't function as well afterward either. In some species, tail loss causes a female to take a year off from reproducing, that metabolic energy presumably going into regrowth instead. But that's a small price to pay for life itself.

Fence lizards are only one of several small lizards commonly found in the Los Angeles basin, and that diversity is growing as new invasive species arrive and establish themselves. My favorite of all the small animals that appear in my backyard is the native southern alligator lizard (*Elgaria multicarinata*), a six-inch lizard with an equally long tail, a gold-scaled body, and a robust head, capable of biting hard but more likely to drop its tail when grabbed by your hand or your cat's jaws. Alligator lizards of various forms occur across the western United States, some of them quite beautiful. In addition to their oversized heads and jaws, they're notable for their long lifespans. Alligator lizards have lived longer than fifteen years in captivity, remarkable for a small reptile. They're also known for their mating habits. It's common in spring to come across a mating pair, the male's massive jaws locked onto the head of the female, their lithe bodies intertwined. These mating episodes can be coital marathons, lasting hours or even days. At some point during this painful-looking process they mate, although the coupling seems to last far longer than necessary for insemination to take place. Other marauding males may clamp their jaws onto the head of the first male, creating a domino effect, perhaps awaiting their chance to wrest the female away from her initial suitor.

Though the fence lizard and alligator lizard are the most widespread and visible Los Angeles lizards, several other species occur in our area. Side-blotched lizards (*Uta stansburiana elegans*) are rarely found in backyards or urban settings, but when you're out hiking a local canyon, they often skitter across the trail. They're similar to fence lizards, at smaller scale, and best known among biologists for their fascinating rock-paper-scissors mating game. My late colleague Barry Sinervo and his colleagues discovered an elaborate male social dynamic in this species, in which different males have different throat colors corresponding to their dominance status. Orange-throated males are dominant to blue-throated males in controlling large territories containing many females, because they're bigger and have higher testosterone levels. But those same dominant orange-throated males lose out to yellow-throated males, which don't control land at all but sneak into orange-throated territories to mate with their females. Meanwhile, blue-throated males get together and cooperate to hold territories, which makes them even more successful breeders than yellow-throats. Sinervo set out to understand how this complex system evolved, and found that the three color morphs have likely existed for eons, but that some morphs have disappeared from some populations. The dominant, most successful morph varied among populations, and also flip-flopped every few years. It appears that the researchers were looking at nascent new species in the early stages of formation, in which the disappearance of a morph might lead to the rapid evolution of the other morphs into separate species. That a little nondescript lizard can teach us big lessons about how the natural world works is yet another reason to take care of the habitat in which they live.

The last native lizard species in the LA basin is the western whip-tail *(Aspidoscelis tigris)*. While it's no larger than an alligator lizard, its long tail—as its name implies—gives it an appearance of larger size and length. A bold pattern of stripes and checkers adds to the illusion of length as it flees danger. Although I've never seen a western whiptail in a local backyard, they're common in the brushy areas in and around our local canyons. My local native plant nursery hosts a population of them.

In addition to native lizard species, a host of nonnative invaders live in the Los Angeles area too. At least five lizard species have arrived in Southern California in the past few decades by various means and established themselves. In some cases, they compete with our native lizards for food and space and may eventually pose a threat to their existence. For example, a few neighborhoods in Los Angeles host populations of green anoles *(Anolis carolinensis)*. These are the little lizards with velvety skins that pet shops have sold for a century, often under the trade name "chameleon," which they are emphatically *not* (actual chameleons are African lizards with protruding eyes, accordion tongues, and feet and tails built for climbing). Green anoles are native to the southeastern United States, where they are extremely common in some areas. In fact, anoles as a group are among the most successful and widespread of all reptiles, occurring across the Caribbean and into Latin America. Green anoles in your backyard are easily identified; they're the only fully emerald-green lizard, at least when they've turned green. Their skin color transforms from bright green to brown throughout the day and night, in tandem with local weather conditions, temperature, and their own activities (unlike many species of true chameleons, whose skin pigment changes rapidly to match their surroundings). Male green anoles also sport a dewlap—an impressive erectable pink throat sac that they use in territorial and mating displays.

A recent arrival to the Los Angeles area threatens to be a widespread lizard here, and may displace some native lizard populations. The Italian wall lizard *(Podarcis siculus)* is a very pretty green-and-gold lizard found all across Italy—the lizards you see basking on stone walls and around vineyards, where they reach an incredible density of thousands per hectare.

According to some accounts, sometime in the mid-1990s a

resident of San Pedro in the Long Beach area returned home from a visit home to Sicily. With him came a handful of the Sicilian variety of wall lizard (*P. s. siculus*), presumably because they would remind him of home. Problem is, those several lizards bred and began spreading out from their point of release. Today they continue to expand their range outward from San Pedro. Greg Pauly, curator of herpetology at the Natural History Museum of Los Angeles County, has been documenting this spread and believes the wall lizards have a negative impact on the native fence lizard population.

We tend to think of geckos as animals from warm climates, and indeed the more than one thousand species of gecko reach their greatest diversity in the tropical regions of Africa and Asia. They range in size from tiny lizards smaller than your pinky finger to giants like the tokay gecko (*Gekko gecko*), a foot-long-plus Asian monster with a loud call and a bite to match, now a common invasive lizard in the Miami area. Some gecko species are famous for their amazing toe grips that allow them to scale smooth vertical surfaces, including glass. The few gecko species native to the United States are secretive, nocturnal desert lizards unseen by most of us. Los Angeles is home to a variety of nonnative geckos that made their way here as ship stowaways or escapees from the pet trade. We are hardly the only American city with invasive geckos: other warm areas like southern Florida and most of the Hawaiian Islands are literally overrun with a plethora of geckos that are native to Asia, Africa, and Madagascar.

In the Los Angeles basin, the Mediterranean house gecko (*Hemidactylus turcicus*) is the species you are most likely to see: small and bumpy skinned, often glued to an exterior wall in the glare of a light, lying in wait to grab an insect meal. These geckos arrived in the United States more than a century ago and have made their way to at least twenty states, as well as to Mexico and the Caribbean.

They are among the most successful of the world's invasive reptiles. Despite their success, they likely don't directly compete for insect food with our local Los Angeles lizard species, since they're nocturnal and arboreal.

A second nonnative gecko in Los Angeles, the Indo-Pacific gecko (*Hemidactylus garnotii*) is a smooth-skinned counterpart to the Mediterranean species. This Southeast Asian lizard is established in Hawai'i and parts of the southern United States. Like Mediterranean geckos, it's seen at night hunting under lights. The most noteworthy thing about this species is that all individuals are female. They reproduce parthenogenetically without the benefit of (or need for) a male's sperm. Only a handful of animals have adapted this evolutionary tweak, including some lizards and snakes, and it serves them well in areas where their densities are low and finding mates is difficult. A cousin of the western whiptail, the New Mexican whiptail (*Aspidoscelis neomexicana*) has the same adaptation, but in that species there is a chromosomal tweaking and multiplying during sex cell division, such that female DNA actually has variety. Offspring are entirely female, but the shuffling of their DNA means that they are not clones of one another. As unusual as it is, parthenogenesis even occurs sometimes in the mighty Komodo dragon (*Varanus komodoensis*) the world's largest lizard, for whom reproduction without sex may well serve a dragon swimming from its tiny island home to a nearby island where mates are few and far between.

Most of our local native lizard species have adapted well to the conversion of their arid canyon-and-brush world to well-watered suburbia of groomed gardens and lawns. Eco-conscious homeowners can help them by putting out rocks for basking spots and brush piles for shelter, and by replacing sterile lawns with a more diverse ecosystem of wildflowers and perennial shrubs.

25

The Family Tortoise

Tortoises do not occur naturally in the Los Angeles basin. The closest they come is roughly eighty kilometers (fifty miles) away from downtown Los Angeles in the Palmdale area, where a few have survived amid the sprawl extending from LA. To find a healthy wild population, one must travel closer to a hundred fifty kilometers to the Barstow area. There lives the Mojave desert tortoise (*Gopherus agassizii*), a denizen of furnace-hot regions of southeastern California, southernmost Nevada, and bits of southwestern Utah and northwestern Arizona. Mojave desert tortoises are wonderfully adapted animals to southwestern deserts, although their habitat was historically more of a grassland before an earlier incarnation of climate change rendered the region uninhabitable except by the hardiest desert creatures and plants.

Even people who hate reptiles tend to love tortoises. They are hard not to like: a dinosaurian creature whose E.T.-like face and utterly placid nature evoke a sense of Zen wisdom of the ages. In fact, most tortoises encountered in the desert are not particularly old. Although their theoretical maximum lifespan is well over one hundred, most die decades earlier due to the many vicissitudes of a hard life: disease, predators, flooded burrows, falls from cliffs, or other mishaps. A thirty-year-old tortoise has reached a relatively ripe age, and that's without humans making life much more difficult.

Although we think of desert tortoises as supremely adapted to life in a scalding-hot climate, and marvel at their ability to go without drinking water for many months on end, the reality is a bit different. Desert tortoises spend 95 percent of their lives in a far more equable microclimate, deep enough in their underground burrows that temperatures hover around seventy degrees Fahrenheit, while just a few meters above, the surface broils at well over one hundred degrees. In addition, subsurface temperatures and humidity are more consistent than those aboveground, reducing the risk of dehydration. With rare exceptions, tortoises venture aboveground only in early morning or late afternoon to search for the food plants that sustain them, to find a mate in the spring, or to challenge a rival male who's too inquisitive about their burrow. A few hours on the surface in summer would be as dangerous to a tortoise as it would be to an unprepared human. In the heat of summer and the cold of winter, a tortoise doesn't leave its burrow at all, staying put underground except on occasional warm, sunny days.

Even with the livable microclimate they create underground, tortoises still endure tremendous water deprivation. They store water, along with body waste, in their oversized urinary bladders. During extremely dry periods they may lose nearly half their body weight, during which time their overall water volume also decreases by more than half. In such water crunches, the concentration of urine in the bladder reaches extreme levels. When rains return tortoises emerge from their burrows to gulp water and void the most concentrated urine from their bodies.

The Los Angeles suburbs are full of tortoises. No one knows how many there are, but a reasonable estimate is in the tens of thousands. A recent estimate in the Las Vegas area, where there are far fewer households, was well over one hundred thousand captive desert tortoises. Their very unnatural habitat is backyards, and occasionally living rooms.

The chelonian most commonly kept in Los Angeles backyards is California's only native tortoise, the Mojave desert tortoise. There was a time a generation or two ago when it was a tradition to pick up a tortoise on a family camping trip to the desert. Back in Los Angeles, the uprooted animal amicably settled down to a life of grazing the backyard grass and weeds. But desert tortoises are powerful diggers, easily capable of burrowing under most fences and walls. Those that didn't dig their way to freedom to wander the neighborhood became lifelong pets, often outliving their owners. Like a family keepsake, they were passed to children and grandchildren. Sometimes a pair would lay eggs and there would be a next generation of captive-bred desert tortoises roaming the yard.

Backyard tortoises live a life utterly unlike their wild counterparts. They are surrounded by a cornucopia of food: lawn grass, weeds, and leaves, not to mention the veggies and fruit their owners give them with the best intentions. Tortoises spent millions of years eking out a harsh existence on scarce desert plants, with a spring bloom of flowers to feast on. They are not adapted to thrive on a diet that contains more than minimal water, or watery foods like lettuce, or acidic tomatoes. They'll survive on this diet—they're tortoises, and toughness is a long-evolved trait—but they won't live out their potentially long lifespans. Naive owners sometimes even feed cat or dog food or table scraps to their tortoises, an unspeakably unsuitable diet for their bodies, with a level of protein and fat comparable to shoving a few steaks into your mouth every day. In some tortoise species, an overabundance of protein in the diet, combined with other factors, can produce freakish growth abnormalities: shells with pyramidal peaks in each scute, or worse. Even lawn grass is too nutritious to be an ideal year-round diet for a species adapted to the natural boom and bust cycles of the desert.

After decades of pet collection from the wild, it became clear that desert tortoise numbers were plummeting. The threats are many. Their desert lands have been degraded or outright destroyed by development and uncontrolled off-road recreational vehicles. As human development encroaches on the desert, scavengers like coyotes and ravens follow, and their booming numbers make them "subsidized" predators that rely on human detritus while also hunting baby tortoises. Even invasive fire ants kill baby tortoises.

Finally, in 1990, the Mojave desert tortoise was given federal protection under the US Endangered Species Act, allowing the government to restrict land use that was harmful to increasingly precarious tortoise populations. Then the law of unintended consequences took over. Many desert tortoise owners released their long-term pets back into the desert, thinking they were doing a good deed. What happened next depends on which expert you listen to. A widespread respiratory disease outbreak occurred among many wild desert tortoises, the source of which may have been the formerly captive tortoises. Bubbly nasal discharges were a giveaway, and cultures taken from the nasal passages often showed serious levels of *Mycoplasma* bacteria. If housed in captivity in proximity to infected tortoises, desert tortoises often became infected. Some areas of the California desert saw tortoise populations crash in the years following the federal listing. While not all experts agreed on the link between pet and wild tortoises, the devastation was indisputable.

Today, bacterial plagues are still a conservation issue, but other problems have taken the fore. As I noted earlier, raven numbers are ever increasing in the desert, and are a scourge to baby tortoises. So is habitat loss. Endless battles are fought over land use in the desert. The eastern Mojave region of Southern California, which seemed so vast and wild a generation ago, is shrinking due to human encroachment every year, and the areas that offer sanctuary to tortoises and other desert animals shrink with it. Tortoise densities in the Mojave have plummeted from more than a hundred animals per square kilometer in the recent past, to only two or three today. In just the past twenty years, an estimated one hundred thousand tortoises have been lost, representing nearly a third of the remaining population. A recovery plan by the US Fish and Wildlife Service was created in the 1990s, updated in 2011, that attempted to protect habitat and tortoises that local and federal government agencies were failing to protect. Nevertheless, tortoise populations remain in steep decline across their range and are now considered in critical danger of extinction.

Meanwhile, back in Los Angeles suburbia, the captive population of desert tortoises continues to grow. In some cases, Mojave desert tortoises that are uprooted by the construction of a highway or shopping mall can be translocated and released back into the wild elsewhere, but most of the time these animals end up in rescue centers. Tortoises seized from those who possess them illegally also end up in rescue centers, as do tortoises injured by cars or backyard escapees brought to local animal shelters. These tortoises become wards of the US Fish and Wildlife Service and state wildlife protection agencies. The goal of such programs is to discourage people from simply dumping unwanted pet tortoises into the desert, where they might introduce pathogens to wild populations, and also to house and care for the hundreds of thousands of wild tortoises that end up in rescue centers and subsequently cannot be returned to the wild.

Under the appropriate authority, a number of rescue groups adopt out the animals to households. The animals, protected under state law, remain the property of the state wildlife agency, but they become the forever pets of the adopter. In Arizona, Nevada, and Utah, the number of tortoises available for adoption usually outnumbers potential adopters. But in Southern California, with its huge human population, adopters outnumber tortoises. Adoption groups limit tortoises to one per household and forbid keeping a male-female pair, but many homes have older tortoises that were grandfathered in before the current protections were enacted in the 1990s. And plenty of tortoise owners are off the adoption grid, sometimes with ten or more tortoises that breed more tortoises. Breeding tortoises is technically illegal—a burgeoning captive population is already a problem—but that rule is widely ignored.

In the wild, these icons of the California desert continue to decline. The International Union for the Conservation of Nature (IUCN), the world's largest conservation monitoring body, officially listed the Mojave desert tortoise as Vulnerable to Extinction in the 1990s, but recently it upgraded the species' status to Critically Endangered. It is at significant risk of extinction in the wild in the coming years unless action is taken to protect both habitat and animals.

The rapid drop in tortoise numbers isn't due only to environmental issues. What we currently call the Mojave desert tortoise was once lumped together with the desert tortoises farther east in Arizona and farther south into Sonora, Mexico. But recent genetic studies have shown that there are three distinguishable species in that complex, and so they have been split: A substantial portion of what used to be called North American desert tortoises (*G. agassizii*) is now recategorized as the Sonoran desert tortoise (*G. morafkai*) in Arizona and the thornscrub tortoise (*G. evgoodei*) in Mexico. Thus, the effective population of Mojave desert tortoises plummeted overnight. Recognizing three species instead of just one reflects biological reality, but at the same time the conservation struggle for each of them has been instantly compounded by their now-fragmented species' numbers.

Among the several exotic species of tortoise that are widely available in pet stores and online, the most common is the so-called sulcata or African spurred tortoise (*Geochelone sulcata*). These tortoises are sold to unsuspecting turtle lovers for as little as fifty dollars. Sulcatas are rapacious eaters, fanatical diggers, and will within a few years grow to gargantuan sizes. A large male sulcata will, at twenty or so years old, approach two feet in length and weigh two hundred pounds (eighty kilograms). Males can be highly aggressive to other tortoises of their and other species, ramming them mercilessly. They also breed prolifically. Sulcatas can be responsive, intelligent backyard pets, but owners typically abandon them as they outgrow their yards.

It is entirely possible that the captive population of our local desert tortoises will someday outnumber that of its wild brethren. If that happens, it's unlikely that the trend will reverse itself, as their desert habitat shrinks at the hands of our greed for land to build on and play on. This iconic desert animal, perhaps the most intensively studied and protected reptile on Earth, may have no future in Southern California except as a backyard pet.

26

Worms, Snails, and Other Creepy-Crawlies

In winter, my compost bin is a mass of wriggling worms. The summertime dry grass and discarded veggies turn to organic mush in winter rains, destined for my garden to aerate and enrich the soil. But earthworms wriggle their way up from the soil beneath in winter to help turn the refuse into something truly valuable, albeit a bit gross. The worms are small and thin and red, and they seem as natural and native to our backyards as the grass and sunshine. Little do most homeowners know that there are hundreds of species of earthworms in the world, and often several just in our backyards. Some species live in deep tunnels in the soil (such as the large nightcrawlers, *Lumbricus terrestris*), others are just below the surface, and still others occupy the leaf litter underfoot. In the Los Angeles area, we had several native species, now replaced by earthworms introduced from other parts of the world. European, Latin American, and Asian nonnative species that thrive in human-altered places like suburbia have largely displaced our native earthworms, except in areas still undeveloped and far from roads and houses.

There's a reason that the non-gardeners among us tend to see earthworms only after a rainstorm. First, rain brings the worms from their soil homes, likely not because they are drowning, as we often think, but because they are in search of mates, which are easier to find on the surface than in the soil. Once in daylight, light-sensitive cells in the worm's head are triggered and they writhe furiously on your sidewalk or lawn. It's common to see a pair joined by their light-colored mucous bands, the clitellas, which hold their reproductive organs, and through which they will swap sperm—earthworms being hermaphroditic. Each partner will then lay egg cocoons, from which hatch tiny versions of their parents. Because suburban lawns and gardens are well watered all year round, worms' normal spring breeding season has been extended to the entire year.

Earthworm farming is big business, both in the sale of worms for home gardens and compost bins, and in the sale of the bins themselves. Only a few species are ideal composters; the red worm (*Eisenia fetida*) is the species most often used in composting, native to Europe and adapted to chewing its way through the layer of leaf litter that coats the ground. A handful of good compost may contain dozens of red worms of all ages and sizes. During a rainy winter, my compost bin is seething with worms, pill bugs, and more; by summer, months of dry heat have driven the worms underground. As long as the compost bin contains only plant material (paper towels, hair, and other household refuse are fair composting game too), the bin will be self-sustaining with moderate care and the abundant help of earthworms, which pass organic material through their long digestive tracts, creating a nutrient-rich part of the leaf litter that we can use to feed our gardens. Earthworm species that live farther down in the soil also munch organic material as they burrow through it, and their excrements are called castings. These castings make good soil fertilizer. Nightcrawlers—the big bait worms—and other larger species that live even deeper in the soil are typically sought as composters, simply because they eat organic soil but not surface organics.

Nonnative earthworms perform the same functions in your garden soil as natives would, so all is good, right? In fact, nonnative earthworms alter the natural soil texture and density by munching the leaf litter, and also change the community of microbes and nutrients that call it home, thereby impacting delicate plants and small animals that require a narrow range of soil conditions. Earthworm-wrought ecological alterations can allow invasive plants to take hold and outcompete the native plant community. Invasive European earthworms have been linked to the spread of invasive plants and a decline in native plants in forests of the eastern United States, which has no native earthworms. Invasive earthworms are considered by conservationists to be an underappreciated threat to biodiversity on a global scale. On the Channel Islands earthworms don't naturally occur, but Eurasian and South American species have been unintentionally introduced, causing concerns about the future of the soil ecosystem there.

We tend to lump together all the little creepy-crawly creatures in our yards, thinking of earthworms, slugs, snails, and others as closely related. In fact, nothing could be further from the truth. Many of these little creatures are separated by tens of millions of years of evolution. (We do the same thing with tidepool animals, yet sea stars, anemones, and urchins are less related to each other than you are to a frog.) Earthworms and slugs are both mucus-coated invertebrates with a deep evolutionary history as sea creatures. Their ancestors first made the transition to freshwater, and then later to land, or at least moist soil. The two groups have little else in common; they adapted to land in completely separate lineages, through paths not connected for a hundred million years or more.

Slugs and snails are among the most beautiful of small creatures, and for gardeners the most reviled. They can wreak destruction on a vegetable garden in just a few nights, leaving telltale damage to plants that's only visible the following morning, when the perpetrators are back under the flowerpots or boards from whence they came. Snails are basically just slugs with protective shells. The oceans, rivers, and lakes of the world are full of snails, but unlike their cousins the bivalve mollusks—clams, scallops, and mussels—which all remained in the water, the gastropod (stomach-footed) mollusks include many diverse families that made their way to dry land eons ago. They did this by evolving a parallel version of vertebrate lungs: a cavity used as a respiratory chamber. This lung actually evolved first in water, and is still used by all those aquatic snails.

Land snails comprise myriad forms and sizes, from the size of your fist to smaller than a baby's fingernail, and live almost everywhere in the world. They managed to colonize habitats from swamps to near-deserts, with their amazing shell and tendency to estivate—to hibernate in hot weather—protecting them from drying out in dry seasons. A mantle of spongy flesh cloaks the snail's body and protects the mantle cavity in which breathing takes place. The mantle is a huge appendage, the bottom part of which is the snail's "foot," which leaves a thick, slimy mucous trail behind. The slime simultaneously creates a sticky surface on which the snail can adhere, and also lubricates rough surfaces; other snails will follow this slime trail too.

They avoid exposed, windy places to prevent desiccation and cluster together in damp, dark places in the daytime, also to avoid drying out. The snail's head features stalks with light-sensing eyes that help it maintain a day-to-night cycle. Underneath, a radula—a scraping beak full of tiny teeth that is the snail's mouth—efficiently chews its way through plants and fruit and pretty much anything else. Like earthworms, snails and slugs reproduce hermaphroditically.

Slugs are not a group of creatures that all necessarily arose from the same ancestral slug. Instead, our English word *slug* refers to any of several evolutionary lines of creatures whose bodies have converged on a slug-shaped, slimy form. Slugs are more prone to desiccation than land snails, and so are more limited to cool, moist environments, at least in the daytime.

Gardeners in Southern California are all too familiar with our local banded garden slug *(Ambigolimax valentianus)*, which like many other backyard denizens here is not a species native to the United States. Most of those that you encounter in your garden happily bulldozing your plants or sleeping the day away under a flower pot were brought to the US either on purpose or accidentally, made their way into our ecosystems, and are now agricultural pests. The brown garden snail *(Cornu aspersum)*, for instance, was imported to Southern California intentionally a century and a half ago to be raised as escargot. Once liberated, they spread rapidly, replacing native snails. Likewise, the similar milk snail *(Otala lactea)* is well established as an invasive garden pest, abundant and harmful to our native plants. Following the law of unintended consequences, a second nonnative species, the decollate snail *(Rumina decollata)* was imported for the express purpose of preying on brown garden snails, which had already become an agricultural pest. Decollate snails love to eat brown garden snails, but they also relish a variety of other species, including our native endangered snails. In my experience, decollate snails are less common than the ubiquitous brown garden snails. The rotund disc snail (*Discus rotundatus*), a flat, spiral-shelled European snail, also appears in our gardens, as do many other species, from the tiny glass snails (genera *Oxychilus* and *Zonitoides*) to flatcoil (genus *Polygyra*) and grass (genus *Vallonia*) snails. Still other species, both native and introduced, are so small—often the size of a pin head—that you'd have to look very carefully through a handful of leaf litter to locate one.

Slugs are practically as ubiquitous as snails in suburbia, because our lawn sprinklers and general heavy watering allows them to survive in an arid climate. Every gardener has had to cope with introduced greenhouse slugs (*Ambigolimax valentiana* and *Milax gagates*) ravaging seedling tomatoes and zucchinis. The damage they do can kill plants that are themselves invasive, perhaps providing some balance to our bizarrely contrived ecosystem. But the invasive plants that are frequent slug food have themselves replaced our native species. And some ecosystems that have been less affected by invasives, like the Channel Islands, have myriad plant species that are highly vulnerable to invasive snails and slugs.

While slugs and snails have predators in our Los Angeles ecosystem—many birds eat them, as do raccoons and skunks and opossums—they nevertheless remain abundant and destructive to both introduced and native plants. Baits can be put near their favored plants in the garden or on the patio—whether commercial snail and slug baits or dishes of beer; the sugar attracts them. Salt is death to snails and slugs, and encircling a favorite plant with salt will keep them at bay, though it takes a lot vigilance and a lot of salt. The best solution may be just a regular nocturnal hunting expedition for the ravagers; especially on warm, moist evenings they can be plucked off the plants after dark.

Not all the commonly encountered crawling creatures in our gardens are mollusks or segmented worms. Pill bugs—the garden roly-polies of our childhood, also known as woodlice—are isopods, and taken more broadly, Arthropods, the group that includes crabs and shrimp. Most isopods are marine creatures that live in the sea or in coastal environments, likely the single origin for all the modern forms. Unlike earthworms and slugs, pill bugs have a hard segmented exoskeleton that has allowed them to survive in environments that are not moist at all; some species live in near-desert habitats. The familiar common pill bug *(Armadillidium vulgare)*, which rolls itself into a ball when disturbed, is one of the most abundant creatures in North America, reaching densities in the thousands per square meter in our garden soil. Each of its seven body segments possesses a set of tiny legs, and gills underneath its body carry out respiration. A pair of antennae and multiple layers of mouthparts, much like a crab's or lobster's, are usually hidden. Pill bugs are harmless, eating organic matter in the soil. They are also, like so many other inhabitants of suburbia, nonnatives, invading our ecosystems from Europe and the Mediterranean. A second European introduction, the common rough woodlouse *(Porcellio scaber)* also inhabits suburban and nearby woodlot areas in the Los Angeles basin. Both have been in North America for hundreds of years, and presumably stowed away on plants brought here by colonists. Since then, they have spread from coast to coast, and colonized habitats from backyard compost bins to arid canyons and beyond.

Pill bugs are a rare case of an introduced species that has no documented harmful effect on its ecosystem. They help to break down nutrients in the soil in their role as scavengers and decomposers. Like earthworms, their excrement is consumed by soil bacteria and fungi, which benefits plants. They have also been shown to help break down the heavy metals that occur in many garden soils, promoting soil health.

Creepy-crawlies are underfoot everywhere we tread, churning the detritus of a suburban ecosystem into something far more useful: energy and food. The next time you see earthworms wriggling on the sidewalk after a rain, think about them in that light.

CONCLUSION

As I walk out my front door on a recent morning, the crystal blue sky is broken by a flock of fifty or more big green parrots. They are red-headed Amazons, the common large parrot in the San Gabriel Valley. They careen into the trees at my curb and start a group chatter that would make conversation difficult on the ground below. I stand underneath, admiring their emerald mantles with flashes of red, the darkening sky with a still-setting full moon behind them. As I watch the parrots eat and quarrel and socialize, my eye is distracted by something walking past me on the ground. It's a lone peacock, a magnificent male with a long train of feathers. He eyes me as he passes a few feet away. The sidewalk is, in his view, his space. Two bird species that hail from opposite sides of the world share space in my little suburb.

"Sharing space" is a very simplistic way of describing an ecosystem. With their myriad organic components—soil, plants, animals, plus the climate that ultimately regulates them—natural ecosystems are almost incomprehensibly complex. A tropical forest's ecological webs make a major urban center look simple by comparison. An ecosystem comprises the flow of energy, the effects of yearly variations in climate, and the living organisms that compose it. Ecologists have studied different kinds of ecosystems—from deserts to arctic tundras to rainforests—for decades to understand how they work, and how human activities affect them, often in harmful, disruptive ways. Our Los Angeles suburban/urban ecosystem is fundamentally different from a natural ecosystem. The moving parts did not evolve together; a significant number of the animals and plants arrived from elsewhere—many unintentionally, and a few intentionally. It is, as I've described in this book, a beautiful but largely nonfunctional landscape, hollow in the sense that the platforms on which an ecosystem should be built, the insects and plants, have been largely replaced by nonnatives.

Does that mean that our local ecosystem is just an environmental hodge-podge whose components have no points of intersection? Not exactly. Consider the case of the coyotes, which are native to our area but have altered their habits to adjust to a human-dominated world in which domestic cats, nonnative rodents, and human detritus are major food items. Or feral cats, which are introduced, of course, but among the most important—and devastating—predators on songbirds in all suburban ecosystems.

In other cases, native species have had their ecologies fundamentally changed by human activity. Hummingbirds that used to migrate no longer do, because of the super-supply of backyard sugar-water feeders that have replaced the flowers they search for. The abundance of feeders and garden flowers has meanwhile expanded the range of some hummingbird species, like the Allen's hummingbird, from the coastal regions inland. So, understanding our local human-altered ecosystem requires understanding each plant and animal species, along with the many, diverse ways in which they interrelate.

The ways in which exotic animals and plants impact an ecosystem are often dramatically different from what anyone predicted. Sometimes exotic species run amok and crowd out local natives, and sometimes they fail to make a toehold at all. Some outcomes seem predictable with 20/20 hindsight; others were completely unforeseen. It should have been obvious that eastern fox squirrels could conquer the Los Angeles basin; they had already made Midwestern suburbia their bailiwick. But when European starlings and European house sparrows were released in the New York City area in the 1800s, few would have foreseen the ubiquity and sheer numbers of the rodents a century later. I doubt the early importers of peafowl foresaw them becoming neighborhood fixtures across Los Angeles. Feral house cat predation on rodents has always been welcomed, but allowed to roam freely in a semi-wild state, they have also slaughtered countless small birds and animals. Few gave serious thought to the possibility that the palm trees gracefully lining our streets would someday become arborea non grata from an environmental standpoint, or that our magnificent valley and Engelmann oaks, so abundant that they were wantonly cut down to make room for subdivisions, could be threatened with local extirpation.

Of course, environmental ethics have changed dramatically from a century ago when much of Los Angeles was being developed, and many saw wildness as something to be tamed or destroyed. Instead of shooting all the local bears and coyotes, we now try to find ways to coexist with them, embracing them as neighbors with a right to live their lives in peace.

Our longing for a connection with Nature hangs in a strange and contradictory balance with our desire to keep it at arm's length. We want it, but not *too much* of it. A city park, with its expanse of carefully mown green grass, is a sanitized version of a wild meadow or a curated forest, and has a powerful appeal as a restorative treatment for the soul. But the first bee sting or poison oak rash makes us want to clear the brush around our homes and keep our kids out of the garden. We crave a walk in a local canyon, but the sight of a coyote or rattlesnake makes us question whether this is a safe place to raise our children or walk our dogs.

For many, there's a deep attraction to parrots and peafowl in the front yard and bears drinking from the swimming pool. These creatures have not stayed in their lane, ecologically speaking. The gift they bring us is undeniably powerful. Restoring biodiversity, from building freeway corridors that enable the natural movements of mountain lions and other wildlife, to planting pocket parks with little patches of native plants, nurtures us. There are psychological benefits to having Nature close at hand.

Coexisting with wildlife takes commitment. It takes dedicated individuals to do the work of restoring habitat, plus money and time and patience to overcome physical and bureaucratic obstacles. It is by no means certain that we will be able to preserve the small population of mountain lions in Los Angeles; they are one epidemic or a few freeway collisions away from extirpation. But if remnant habitat is protected and access created, new lions could eventually make their way into our area to replace those lost. There is potential for a population of apex predators to live in our midst in perpetuity, astounding for a place as urban as Los Angeles.

Predicting the future is, however, a fool's errand. We can predict the next ten or twenty years with some accuracy, and we can make plausible speculations about the next fifty years. But it's dicey beyond just a few decades. We can do what we will to manage our ecosystem, but some events will play a crucial role in determining what happens, from changing seasons due to climate change, to our increasingly disastrous wildfire cycles, to the growth and spread of humanity.

Still, there is so much that we can do to make our landscapes more functional from an ecological perspective. The near future in Southern California is one in which exotic plants and animals will continue to play an outsized role in shaping our views of Nature, but cultivating native plants and habitats can create a healthier balance. One of the special attractions of life in Los Angeles is that we can savor all the cultural benefits of the big city while encountering a bear, coyote, or peacock in the neighborhood—and experience wild, undeveloped Nature only a short walk or drive away. For everyone's sake, it should remain that way.

Acknowledgments

During the COVID-19 pandemic, I sat down to write a book that I had always wanted but could never find the time to write. Suddenly, on a badly timed sabbatical from teaching at my university and with all international travel canceled, I had the time. I drew on three decades living in the San Gabriel Valley just north of Los Angeles, and the many interactions I've had with our local animals and plants, as well as with local people who passionately love and passionately hate them. The result is this book.

Unnatural Habitat is part of a literature on a more eco-conscious, eco-ethical view of urban and suburban life that has emerged over the past decade or more. This movement was long overdue, and California's episodic drought, made increasingly severe by climate change, is part what's causing our changing ethic. But I hope there's more to it: that people are finally realizing that their suburban haunts should fit into the natural local landscape, not simply reflect the landscape they grew up valuing.

I'm grateful to the people and institutions that have helped to mold my own changing worldview about Los Angeles suburbia. The staff of the Natural History Museum of Los Angeles County have been an inspiration for me over the years, and I thank Carol Bornstein and her coauthors Bart O'Brien and David Fross for her influential books about native California plants, and my colleagues Greg Pauly and Kimball Garrett for their work on the native and nonnative wildlife of Los Angeles. I'm also grateful to the dedicated staff of the Theodore Payne Foundation for Wild Flowers and Native Plants for educating me for more than twenty-five years about the value and uses of myriad native Southern California plants. The Payne Foundation's work has raised public awareness and certainly contributed to the growing number of home owners who have ripped out all or part of their lawns to plan appropriately drought-tolerant plants that provide food for native insects and other animals.

For their help with discussing the issues raised in this book, and in some cases for reading the text and offering critiques, I am grateful to many friends, colleagues and neighbors past and present, especially John Allen, Donald Burrill, Sheila Carr, Rebecca Davis, Barbara Eisenstein, Diane Link, Erin Moore, Dan Parada, Stephanie Sheffield, Tanja Sterrmann, and the Wilkins family. For her global work in raising environmental consciousness, and for her role in my own development as a scientist, I once again thank Jane Goodall.

I am grateful to my longtime colleague, coauthor, and friend Dr. Maddalena Bearzi for her help in publishing this book, and especially for contributing the illustrations that accompany the text. For their editing skills and editorial advice, I thank Marthine Satris, Emmerich Anklam, and Molly Woodward of Heyday.

As always, I thank my supportive family: Gaelen, Marika, and Adam.

Further Reading

Introduction

Bossard, C. C., J. M. Randall, and M. C. Hoshovsky. *Invasive Plants of California's Wildlands*. Berkeley, CA: University of California Press, 2000.

Holing, D. *California Wild Lands*. San Francisco: Chronicle Books, 1988.

Knapp, R. A. "Non-native trout in natural lakes of the Sierra Nevada: an analysis of their distribution and impacts on native aquatic biota." *Sierra Nevada Ecosystem Project: Final report to Congress,* vol. III, *Assessments and scientific basis for management options,* 363–407. Davis: University of California, Centers for Water and Wildland Resources, 1996.

Tallamy, D. W. *Nature's Best Hope*. Portland, OR: Timber Press, 2019.

1. Palms Up, and Down

Gibbons, M. *Palms*. Seacaucus, NJ: Chartwell Books, Inc., 1993.

2. Winged Gemstones

Clark, C. J., D. O. Elias, and R. O. Prum. "Aeroelastic flutter produces hummingbird feather songs." *Science* 333, no. 6048 (2011): 1430–33. https://doi.org/10.1126/science.1205222.

Pyke, G. H. "Optimal foraging in hummingbirds: testing the marginal value theorem." *American Zoologist* 18, no. 4 (1978): 739–52.

Rico-Guevara, A. and M. A. Rubega. "The hummingbird tongue is a fluid trap, not a capillary tube." *Proceedings of the National Academy of Sciences* 108, no. 23 (2011): 9356–60. https://doi.org/10.1073/pnas.1016944108.

3. Painted Beauties among the Flowers

Albeck-Ripka, L. "California's western monarch butterflies are making a comeback." *New York Times*, December 3, 2021.

Crone, E. E. and C. B. Schulz. "Resilience or catastrophe? A possible state change for monarch butterflies in western North America." *Ecology Letters* 24, no. 8 (2021): 1533–38. https://doi.org/10.1111/ele.13816.

Heath, F. *An Introduction to Southern California Butterflies*. Missoula, MT: Mountain Press Publishing Company, 2004.

Malcolm, S. B. "Milkweeds, monarch butterflies and the ecological significance of cardenolides." *Chemoecology* 5, no. 3 (1994): 101–17.

4. Peafowl Rule This Roost

Dakin, R. and R. Montgomerie. "Peahens prefer peacocks displaying more eyespots, but rarely." *Animal Behaviour* 82, no. 1 (2011): 21–28. https://doi.org/10.1016/j.anbehav.2011.03.016.

Dakin, R. and R. Montgomerie. "Eye for an eyespot: how iridescent plumage ocelli influence peacock mating success." *Behavioral Ecology* 24, no. 5 (2013): 1048–57. https://doi.org/10.1093/beheco/art045.

Darwin, C. *The Descent of Man, and Selection in Relation to Sex.* London: John Murray, 1871.

Kessler, M. "Who's been killing the feral peacocks of Palos Verdes?" *Los Angeles Magazine*, January 5, 2016. https://www.lamag.com /longform/whos-been-killing-the-feral-peacocks-of-palos-verdes/

Yorzinski, J. L., G. L. Patricelli, J. S. Babcock, J. M. Pearson, and M. L. Platt. "Through their eyes: selective attention in peahens during courtship." *Journal of Experimental Biology* 216, no. 13 (2013): 3035–46. https://doi.org/10.1242/jeb.087338.

5. Cats Great and Small

Beier, P. and R. F. Noss. "Do habitat corridors provide connectivity?" *Conservation Biology* 12, no. 6 (1998): 1241–52.

Gustafson, K. D., R. B. Gagne, T. W. Vickers, S. P. D. Riley, C. C. Wilmers, V. C. Bleich, B. M. Pierce, M. Kenyon, T. L. Drazanovich, J. A. Sikich, W. M. Boyce, and H. B. Ernest. "Genetic source-sink dynamics among naturally structured and anthropogenically fragmented puma populations." *Conservation Genetics* 20, no. 2 (2019): 215–27. https://doi.org/10.1007/s10592-018-1125-0.

Morrison, S. A. and W. M. Boyce. "Conserving connectivity: some lessons from mountain lions in southern California." *Conservation Biology* 23, no. 2 (2009): 275–85. https://doi.org/10.1111 /j.1523-1739.2008.01079.x.

Riley, S. P. D., J. P. Pollinger, R. M. Sauvajot, E. C. York, C. Bromley, T. K. Fuller, and R. K. Wayne. "A southern California freeway is a physical and social barrier to gene flow in carnivores." *Molecular Ecology* 15, no. 7 (2006): 1733–41. https://doi.org/10.1111 /j.1365-294X.2006.02907.x.

Serieys, L. E. K., A. Lea, J. P. Pollinger, S. P. D. Riley, and R. K. Wayne. "Disease and freeways drive genetic change in urban bobcat populations." *Evolutionary Applications* 8, no. 1 (2015): 75-92. https://doi.org/10.1111/eva.12226.

6. The Spectacle

Forshaw, J. *Parrots of the World*, 2nd ed. Melbourne: Landsdowne Editions, 1978.

The California Parrot Project. https://www.californiaparrotproject.org.

7. Wily and Wildly Successful

Castelló, J. R. *Canids of the World*. Princeton, NJ: Princeton University Press, 2018.

Flores, D. *Coyote America*. New York: Basic Books, 2016.

Larson, R. N., J. L. Brown, T. Karels, and S. P. D. Riley. "Effects of urbanization on resource use and individual specialization in coyotes *(Canis latrans)* in southern California." *PLoS One* 15, no. 2 (2020): https://doi.org/10.1371/journal.pone.0228881.

Newsome, S. D., H. M. Garbe, E. C. Wilson, and S. D. Gehrt. "Individual variation in anthropogenic resource use in an urban carnivore." *Oecologia* 178, no. 1 (2015): 115–28. http://www.jstor.org/stable/43672010.

Ohio State University and World Science Staff. "Thriving under our noses, stealthily: coyotes." *World Science*, January 5, 2006, https://web.archive.org/web/20060114082304/http://www.world-science.net/othernews/060105_coyotefrm.htm.

White, L. A. and S. D. Gehrt. "Coyote attacks on humans in the United States and Canada." *Human Dimensions of Wildlife* 14, no. 6 (2009): 419–32. https://doi.org/10.1080/10871200903055326.

8. Beloved, Cuddly Killers

Doherty, T. S., A. S. Glen, D. G. Nimmo, E. G. Ritchie, and C. R. Dickman. "Invasive predators and global biodiversity loss." *Proceedings of the National Academy of Sciences* 113, no. 40 (2016): 11261–65. https://doi.org/10.1073/pnas.1602480113.

Feral Cat Caretakers' Coalition. "Mission Statement and Introduction." Feral Cat Caretakers' Coalition, 2003. https://web.archive.org/web/20130209031633/http://feralcatcaretakers.org/Overview/Mission.html.

Longcore, T., C. Rich and L. M. Sullivan. "Critical assessment of claims regarding management of feral cats by trap-neuter-return." *Conservation Biology* 23, no. 4 (2009): https://doi.org/10.1111/j.1523-1739.2009.01174.x.

Loss, S. R., T. Will, and P. P. Marra. "The impact of free-ranging domestic cats on wildlife of the United States." *Nature Communications* 4, no. 1396 (2013). https://doi.org/10.1038/ncomms2380.

9. Little Chewers

Richards, A. "Rats? In my house? Say it ain't so." *Los Angeles Magazine*, February 14, 2017.

Schwan, T. G., D. Thompson, and B. C. Nelson. "Fleas on roof rats in six areas of Los Angeles County, California: their potential role in the transmission of plague and murine typhus to humans." *American Journal of Tropical Medicine and Hygiene* 34, no. 2 (1985): 372–79.

10. Don't Let the Green Grass Fool You

Bornstein, C., D. Fross, and B. O'Brien. *California Native Plants for the Garden.* Los Olivos, CA: Cachuma Press, 2005.

Bornstein, C., D. Fross, and B. O'Brien. *Reimagining the California Lawn.* Los Olivos, CA: Cachuma Press, 2011.

Eisenstein, B. *Wild Suburbia*. Berkeley, California: Heyday, 2016.

Munz, P. A. *Introduction to California Spring Wildflowers*. Berkeley, CA: University of California Press, 2004.

Schmidt, M. G. and K. L. Greenberg. *Growing California Native Plants*, 2nd ed. Berkeley, CA: University of California Press, 2012.

11. All That Rattles and Slithers

Hubbs, B. *Common Kingsnakes*. Tempe, AZ: Tricolor Books, 2009.

Klauber, L. *Rattlesnakes: Their Habits, Life Histories, and Influences on Mankind*. Berkeley, CA: University of California Press, 1956.

Morandi, N., and J. Williams. "Snakebite injuries: Contributing factors and intentionality of exposure." *Wilderness and Environmental Medicine* 8, no. 3 (1997): 152–55.

Spano, S., F. Macias, B. Snowden, and R. Vohra. "Snakebite Survivors Club: Retrospective review of rattlesnake bites in Central California." *Toxicon* 69 (2013): 38–41. https://doi.org/10.1016 /j.toxicon.2012.11.015.

Stebbins, R. C. and S. M. McGinnis. *Field Guide to Amphibians* and *Reptiles of California*. Berkeley, CA: University of California Press, 2012.

Thompson, R. C., A. N. Wright, and H. B. Shaffer. *California Amphibian and Reptile Species of Special Concern*. Oakland, CA: University of California Press, 2016.

12. Arachnophilia

Bond, J. E., N. L. Garrison, C. A. Hamilton, R. L. Godwin, M. Hedin, and I. Agnarsson. "Phylogenomics resolves a spider backbone phylogeny and rejects a prevailing paradigm for orb web evolution." *Current Biology* 24, no. 15 (2014): 1765–71. https://doi.org/10.1016 /j.cub.2014.06.034.

Will, K. *Field Guide to California Insects*. Los Angeles: University of California Press, 2020.

13. The (Once) Mighty Oak

Keator, G. *The Life of an Oak*. Berkeley, CA: Heyday, 1998.

Pavlik, B. M., P. C. Muick, S. G. Johnson, and M. Popper. *Oaks of California*. Los Olivos, CA: Cachuma Press, 1991.

Xu, Q., and J. Greenberg. "LiDAR-Derived Aboveground Biomass and Uncertainty for California Forests, 2005–2014." Oak Ridge, TN: ORNL DAAC, 2018. https://doi.org/10.3334/ORNLDAAC/1537.

Simard, S. W. and D. M. Durall. "Mycorrhizal networks: a review of the extent, function, and importance." *Canadian Journal of Botany* 82, no. 8 (2004): https://doi.org/10.1139/b04-116.

Waddell, K. L.; Barrett, T. M. *Oak woodlands and other hardwood forests of California, 1990s*. Portland, OR: U.S. Department of Agriculture, Forest Service, Pacific Northwest Research Station, 2005. https://doi.org/10.2737/PNW-RB-245.

Yi, X., Z. Wang, C. Liu, G. Liu, and M. Zhang "Acorn cotyledons are larger than their seedlings' need: evidence from artificial cutting experiments." *Scientific Reports* 5, no. 8112: https://doi.org/10.1038/srep08112.

14. Silent Suburbia

Audubon California, California's Common Birds in Decline, https://ca.audubon.org/californias-common-birds-decline.

Garrett, K. L., J. L. Dunn, and B. E. Small. *Birds of Southern California*. Olympia, WA: R. W. Morse Company, 1981.

Higgins, L. M., G. B. Pauly, J. G. Goldman, and C. Hood. *Wild LA*. Portland, OR: Timber Press, 2019.

Pennisi, E. "Three billion North American birds have vanished since 1970, surveys show." *Science*, September 19, 2019. https://doi .org/10.1126/science.aaz5646.

15. Live Forever . . . to Be Poached

McCormick, E. "Stolen Succulents: California hipster plants at center of smuggling crisis." *Guardian*. April 27, 2018. https://www.theguardian .com/environment/2018/apr/27/stolen-succulents-california -hipster-plants-at-center-of-smuggling-crisis.

Thomson, P. H. *Dudleya and Hasseanthus Handbook*. Bonsall, CA: Bonsall Publications, 1993.

16. Pollinators on Life Support

Frankie, G., I. Feng, R. Thorp, J. Pawelek, M. H. Chase, C. C. Jadallah, and M. Rizzardi. "Native and non-native plants attract diverse bees to urban gardens in California." *Journal of Pollination Ecology* 25, no. 3 (2019): https://doi.org/10.26786/1920-7603(2019)505.

Klein, S., C. Pasquaretta, X.J. He, C. Perry, E. Sovik, J. Devaud, A.B. Barron, and M. Lihoreau. "Honey bees increase their foraging performance and frequency of pollen trips through experience." *Scientific Reports* 9, no. 6778 (2019): 6778. https://doi.org/10.1038 /s41598-019-42677-x.

Moisset, B. and S. Buchmann. *Bee Basics: An Introduction to Our Native Bees.* United States Forest Service and USDA Pollinator Partnership, 2012.

Pyke, G. H. "Plant-pollinator co-evolution: it's time to reconnect with optimal foraging theory and evolutionarily stable strategies." *Perspectives in Plant Ecology, Evolution and Systematics* 19 (2016): 70–76. https://doi.org/10.1016/j.ppees.2016.02.004.

Siviter, H., E. J. Bailes, C. D. Martin, T. R. Oliver, J. Koricheva, E. Leadbeater, and M. J. F. Brown. "Agrochemicals interact synergistically to increase bee mortality." *Nature* 596, no. 7872 (2021): 389–92. https://doi.org/10.1038/s41586-021-03787-7.

17. Aerial Hunters in the Backyard

Peeters, H. J. *Raptors of California*. Berkeley: University of California Press, 2005.

Sibley, D. A. *What It's Like to Be a Bird*. New York: Knopf, 2020.

Unwin, M. *The Enigma of the Owl*. New Haven: Yale University Press, 2017.

18. Not Even the Squirrels Belong

Barragan, B. "There is an East Coast/West Coast squirrel war raging in LA." *Curbed Los Angeles*, September 3, 2015, https://la.curbed .com/2015/9/3/9924196/squirrel-battle-east-coast-west-coast -los-angeles.

DeMarco, C., D. S. Cooper, E. Torres, A. Muchlinski, and A. Aguilar. "Effects of urbanization on population genetic structure of western gray squirrels." *Conservation Genetics* 22 (2021): 67-81. https://doi .org/10.1007/s10592-020-01318-x.

King, J. L. "The current distribution of the introduced fox squirrel *(Sciurus niger)* in the greater Los Angeles metropolitan area, and its behavioral interaction with the native western gray squirrel *(Sciurus griseus)*." M.Sc. Dissertation, California State University, Los Angeles.

19. Not Your Average Bear

"Black Bear." California Department of Fish and Wildlife, 2021, https:// wildlife.ca.gov/Conservation/Mammals/Black-Bear.

Murie, A. *The Grizzlies of Mount McKinley*. Washington, DC: U.S. Department of the Interior, National Park Service, 1981.

Vonk, J. and M. J. Beran. "Bears 'count' too: quantity estimation and comparison in black bears, *Ursus americanus*." *Animal Behaviour* 84, no. 1 (2012): 231–38. https://doi.org/10.1016 /j.anbehav.2012.05.001.

20. Love 'Em or Hate 'Em

Bonn, D. "Raccoon roundworms: a threat to human health?" *The Lancet Infectious Diseases* 2, no. 6 (2002): 320. https://doi.org/10.1016/S1473-3099(02)00303-1.

Daniels, S. E., R. E. Fanelli, A. Gilbert, and S. Benson-Amram. "Behavioral flexibility of a generalist carnivore." *Animal Cognition* 22, no. 3 (2019): 387–96. https://doi.org/10.1007/s10071-019-01252-7.

Petit, M. "Raccoon intelligence at the borderlands of science." *Monitor on Psychology* 41, no. 10 (2010): 26–27.

Roussere, G. P., W. J. Murray, C. B. Raudenbush, M. J. Kutilek, D. J. Levee, and K. R. Kazacos. "Raccoon roundworm eggs near homes and risk for larva migrans disease, California communities." *Emerging Infectious Diseases* 9, no. 12 (2003): 1516–22. https://doi.org/10.3201/eid0912.030039.

21. Dumpster Divers and Backyard Stinkers

Bixler, A. and J. Gittleman. "Variation in home range and use of habitat in the striped skunk *(Mephitis mephitis)*." *Journal of Zoology* 251, no. 4 (2000): 525–33. https://doi.org/10.1111/j.1469-7998.2000.tb00808.x.

Feinstein, J. *Field Guide to Urban Wildlife*. Mechanicsburg, PA: Stackpole Books, 2011.

Ferguson, A. W., M. M. McDonough, G. I. Guerra, M. Rheude, J. W. Dragoo, L. K. Ammerman, and R. C. Dowler. "Phyogeography of a widespread small carnivore, the western spotted skunk *(Spilogale gracilis)* reveals temporally variable signatures of isolation across western North America." *Ecology and Evolution* 7, no. 12 (2017): 4229–40. https://doi.org/10.1002/ece3.2931.

Horovitz, I., T. Martin, J. Bloch, S. Ladevéze, C. Kurz, and M. R. Sánchez-Villagra. "Cranial anatomy of the earliest marsupials and the origin of opossums." *PLoS One* 4, no. 12 (2009). https://doi.org/10.1371/journal.pone.0008278.

Ingles, L. G. *Mammals of California*. Palo Alto: Stanford University Press, 1947.

Krause, W. J. and W. A. Krause. *The Opossum: Its Amazing Story*. Columbia MO: Department of Pathology and Anatomical Sciences, School of Medicine, University of Missouri, 2006.

Voss, R. S. and S. A. Jansa. *Opossums: An Adaptive Radiation of New World Marsupials*. Baltimore, MD: Johns Hopkins University Press, 2021.

Wood, W. F. "The History of Skunk Defensive Secretion Research." *The Chemical Educator* 4, no. 2 (1999): 44–50.

Zimmer, C. "Did Grandma Have a Pouch? (And Other Thoughts on the Opossum's Genome)." *National Geographic*, May 9, 2007. https://www.nationalgeographic.com/science/article/did-grandma-have-a-pouch-and-other-thoughts-on-the-opossums-genome.

22. The Smart Ones

Bird, C. D. and N. J. Emery. "Rooks use stones to raise the water level to reach a floating worm." *Current Biology* 19, no. 16 (2009): 1410–14. https://doi.org/10.1016/j.cub.2009.07.033.

Bugnyar, T. "Social cognition in ravens." *Comparative Cognition and Behavior Reviews* 8 (2013): 1–12. https://doi.org/10.3819/ccbr.2013.80001.

Clayton, N. and N. Emery. "Corvid cognition." *Current Biology* 15, no. 3 (2005): 80–81. https://doi.org/10.1016/j.cub.2005.01.020.

Emery, N. and N. S. Clayton. "The mentality of crows: convergent evolution of intelligence in corvids and apes." *Science* 306, no. 5703 (2004): 1903–7. https://doi.org/10.1126/science.1098410.

Tallamy, D. W. "Do alien plants reduce insect biomass?" *Conservation Biology* 18, no. 6 (2004): 1–4. https://www.jstor.org/stable/3589055.

23. Sage Advice

Bornstein, C., D. Fross, and B. O'Brien. *California Native Plants for the Garden*. Los Olivos, CA: Cachuma Press, 2005.

Munz, P. A. *Introduction to California Spring Wildflowers of the Foothills, Valleys and Coast*. Los Angeles: University of California Press, 2004.

Smith, N. *Native Treasures*. Los Angeles: University of California Press, 2006.

24. Lounge Lizards

CaliforniaHerps.com. "Mediterranean Gecko," http://www.californiaherps.com/lizards/pages/h.turcicus.html.

Sinervo, B. and C. M. Lively. "The rock-paper-scissors game and the evolution of alternative male strategies." *Nature* 380, no. 6571 (1996): 240–43. https://doi.org/10.1038/380240a0.

Stebbins, R. C. and S. M. McGinnis. *Field Guide to Amphibians* and *Reptiles of California*. Berkeley, CA: University of California Press, 2012.

Tanner, W. W. and J. M. Hopkin. "Ecology of *Sceloporus occidentalis longipes* Baird and *Uta stanburiana* Baird and Girard on Ranier Mesa, Nevada Test Site, Nye County, Nevada." *Brigham Young University Science Bulletin, Biological Series* 15, no. 4 (1972): 1–39.

25. The Family Tortoise

Brown, M. B., K. H. Berry, I. M. Schumacher, K. A. Nagy, M. M. Christopher, and P. A. Klein. "Seroepidemiology of upper respiratory tract disease in the desert tortoise in the Western Mojave Desert of California." *Journal of Wildlife Diseases* 35, no. 4 (1999): 716–27. https://doi.org/10.7589/0090-3558-35.4.716.

Bulova, S. J. "How temperature, humidity, and burrow selection affect evaporative water loss in desert tortoises." *Journal of Thermal Biology* 27, no. 3 (2002): 175–89. https://doi.org/10.1016/S0306-4565(01)00079-1.

Harless, M. L., A. D. Walde, D. K. Delaney, L. L. Pater, and W. K. Hayes. "Home range, spatial overlap, and burrow use of the desert tortoise in the West Mojave Desert." *Copeia* 2009, no. 2 (2009): 378–89. https://doi.org/10.1643/CE-07-226.

Kristan, W. B. III and W. I. Boarman. "Spatial pattern of risk of common raven predation on desert tortoises." *Ecology* 84, no. 9 (2003): 2432–43. https://doi.org/10.1890/02-0448.

Peterson, C. C. "Anhomeostasis: seasonal water and solute relations in two populations of the desert tortoise *(Gopherus agassizii)* during chronic drought." *Physiological and Biochemical Zoology* 69, no. 6 (1996). https://doi.org/10.1086/physzool.69.6.30164263.

26. Worms, Snails, and Other Creepy-Crawlies

Gundale, M. J. "Influence of exotic earthworms on the soil organic horizon and the rare fern *Botrychium mormo*." *Conservation Biology* 16, no. 6 (2002): 1555–61. https://doi.org/10.1046/j.1523-1739.2002.01229.x.

Nuzzo, V. A., J. C. Maerz, and B. Blossey. "Earthworm invasion as the driving force behind plant invasion and community change in northeastern North American forests." *Conservation Biology* 23, no. 4 (2009): 966–74. https://doi.org/10.1111/j.1523-1739.2009.01168.x.

Paudel, S., G. W. T. Wilson, B. MacDonald, T. Longcore, and S. R. Loss. "Predicting spatial extent of invasive earthworms on an oceanic island." *Biodiversity Research* 22, no. 10 (2016): 1013–23. https://doi.org/10.1111/ddi.12472.

Van Stralen, N. M. "Evolutionary terrestrialization scenarios for soil invertebrates." *Pedobiologia* 87–88 (2021): 150753. https://doi.org/10.1016/j.pedobi.2021.150753.

About the Author

Craig Stanford is a biologist and anthropologist at the University of Southern California. He received his Ph.D. from U.C. Berkeley, and has conducted field research on animal behavior and ecology in remote parts of East Africa, South Asia, and Latin America. Stanford is known for his long-term field research on wild chimpanzees, and for his field studies of endangered turtles and tortoises in Asia and Latin America. He has published eighteen previous books and hundreds of articles about animal behavior and ecology, early human origins, and global environmental issues. He is currently Chair of the I.U.C.N. Tortoise and Freshwater Turtle Specialist Group and travels the world promoting the protection of our shelled friends. Stanford is a longtime resident of the Pasadena area in Southern California and an avid hiker, birder, gardener, and local naturalist.